Praise for TEN STEPS TO RELIEVE ANXIETY

Written in simple, lucid prose, [...] dealing with chronic anxiety will be in [...] ied with this most frustrating of emotic [...] ing case histories, as well as vivid descri[...] [...]chniques applicable, this book will provide anxiety sufferers with a variety of down-to-earth treatment tips till now unavailable from a single source.

—Leon F. Seltzer, PhD
Author of Paradoxical Strategies in Psychotherapy
and blogger for Psychology Today

Dr. Zal's timely book sheds light on a silent problem plaguing today's fast-paced world—the impact of anxiety and stress on overall health. His insight is drawn from many years in clinical practice as an osteopathic psychiatrist and it reflects his genuine desire to help individuals stop suffering and start enjoying life.

—John B. Crosby, JD
Executive Director, American Osteopathic Association

Ten Steps to Relieve Anxiety is a well-written, lucid book that guides the reader through a clear description of and treatment for generalized anxiety dis-order. The case examples are vivid and straightforward. Chapter 11 provides the reader with an extensive, easy-to-understand menu of non-medication treatment options. I highly recommend this book for anyone interested in this disorder.

—William R. Dubin, MD
Professor and Chair, Department of Psychiatry
Temple University School of Medicine

In an era of tension between the brain and mind, Dr. Michael Zal has taken one of the omnipresent feelings of our time—anxiety—and written about how we can grab hold of it. He is well acquainted with the subject from a distinguished career of helping people in the intimate setting of his consulting room, and he shares some of their stories with us in Renaissance fashion: he integrates his knowledge of biological science, clinical medicine and humanism while alleviating their suffering. I think clinicians, patients and their family members will all find his *Ten Steps to Relieve Anxiety* soothing, and will feel more equipped to cope with anxiety when it interferes with our living life fully.

—Andrew I. Smolar, MD
President-Elect, Supervising and Training Analyst
Psychoanalytic Center of Philadelphia

TEN STEPS
TO RELIEVE ANXIETY

TEN STEPS
TO RELIEVE ANXIETY

Refocus, Relax and Enjoy Life

H Michael Zal, DO, FACN, FAPA, Dist

New Horizon Press
Far Hills, New Jersey

Requests for permission should be addressed to:
New Horizon Press
P. O. Box 669
Far Hills, NJ 07931

H Michael Zal, DO, FACN, FAPA, Dist
    Ten Steps to Relieve Anxiety: Refocus, Relax and Enjoy Life

Cover design: Bob Aulicino
Interior design: Susan Sanderson

Library of Congress Control Number: 2013931893

ISBN-13: 978-0-88282-450-5

New Horizon Press

Manufactured in the U. S. A.

17   16   15   14   13   1   2   3   4   5

To Dr. Alice Joy Sheflin Zal
With All My Love to a Very Special Lady

Other Books by H Michael Zal

Panic Disorder: The Great Pretender

The Sandwich Generation:
Caught Between Growing Children and Aging Parents

Dancing With Medusa: A Life In Psychiatry: A Memoir

Author's Note

This book on generalized anxiety disorder (GAD) is unlike other books on the topic that promise a cure. Based on over forty years of experience working with people with anxiety, I maintain that anxiety and worry are due to a genetic vulnerability. GAD may run in families and may grow worse when people are under stress. Its symptoms cannot be eradicated completely. They will always be there to some degree as part of the person's makeup. However, they can indeed be modulated and helped. *Ten Steps to Relieve Anxiety* will show you some proven ways to do this.

Although all the names have been changed, my cases are about actual people and real suffering. I look at clients from a holistic point of view, involving the whole person and his or her life history from childhood to adulthood. I take an eclectic approach to therapy, using aspects of everything from psychoanalytic psychotherapy to cognitive-behavioral therapy. This book explores the skills and insights that you can learn in therapy to help you feel less stressed and anxious and gain more control over your anxiety symptoms and your life. It will also point out common personality traits often seen in anxious people. At times it will take you inside the therapy session and allow you to see the interplay between therapist and client. It will review the various psychiatric medications that are available to help anxiety where appropriate. It is my firm belief that although psychiatric medications can facilitate improvement in mental disorders, it is people working with people on a sustained, long-term basis that is equally or even more important in maintaining recovery and producing emotional growth.

In writing this book, I asked many of my GAD clients to write their responses to two questions: "My anxiety is…?" and "What helps my anxiety?" Some of their honest, heartfelt responses form the authentic vignettes found in each chapter. Specific people have been chosen to illustrate various points relevant to the anxiety-ridden person. The core of each chapter involves their individual life stories. Then both the client and I discuss what we feel has helped his or her anxiety. I have received written permission from each client allowing me to publish their written material and their treatment charts.

If you have anxiety, the stories in this book will show you that you are not alone. They will offer choices that you can use to help yourself be calmer and feel more in control. GAD is not a character flaw. It is a serious and treatable disorder from which millions of adults throughout the world suffer.

Ten Steps to Relieve Anxiety will also be helpful to your family members, friends, caregivers and others who want to understand and support you. It will offer support to professional mental health and medical audiences, social workers, teachers and those who work with the general public and want a better understanding of this common but complex disorder, so they can be of assistance to their patients, clients, students and others.

This book is based on the author's research, personal experiences and clients' real life experiences. In order to protect privacy, names have been changed and identifying characteristics have been altered except for contributing experts. For purposes of simplifying usage, the pronouns his/her and s/he are sometimes used interchangeably. The information contained herein is not meant to be a substitute for professional evaluation and therapy with mental health professionals.

The suggestions in this book as to what can be done to solve your psychological dilemma are only suggestions and options. They should be discussed with your own physician, who knows your medical and family history and your emotional dynamics. Only he or she can put together an individualized treatment plan tailored to your specific medical and psychological needs. If your physical work-up is negative, you may be offered other treatment possibilities, such as therapy and/or medication, to help you feel better and improve the overall quality of your life. Hopefully, your physician will be direct in his or her recommendations but also empathetic and nonjudgmental.

If your physician suggests psychiatric treatment, don't be afraid. If you are troubled and feel that you need help, take the risk and make an appointment. We will not embarrass you. We will not criticize you. We will not diminish you. We are just going to talk. Give it a chance. If you just come and tell us about yourself and your life, whatever has to come out will come to the surface. We can help you connect the dots. You may just find out that you are not alone and perhaps more normal than you think. Hopefully you will realize that your parents did the best that they could and that you have more control over your life than you think. If anything, this experience may start you on the road to emotional maturity, allow you to live up to your full potential and be more content with yourself and your life. Sometimes even the strongest people need someone to talk to, someone who can offer support and light the way. Let a psychiatrist be your guide.

Contents

Part I: Steps to Relieve Anxiety

Part II: Treatment Options

Contents

Part III: High Stress Situations

Foreword

Ten Steps to Relieve Anxiety is the rare book which provides help and understanding to anxious clients, as well as general guidance to their treating psychiatrist. The reader experiences in a very real way how a chronically anxious client suffers and tries to cope with this very disturbing illness known as generalized anxiety disorder (GAD). While reading this book, I could hardly put it down. I was particularly struck by two themes which transcend the whole book and which frequently intersect.

Throughout the entire book, we can actually feel and experience the client's suffering and his or her attempts to deal with the anxiety on his or her own. We also become aware of the fact that most anxious people not only suffer from anxiety and worry, but also from other depressive symptoms. They may, for example, suffer from panic attacks, shyness, compulsiveness and, at least to some degree, depression.

Clients appear on Dr. Zal's doorstep, anxious to an extreme, with very little hope for healthier lives and not knowing what to expect. Whom do they see? A warm, caring, cautious psychiatrist, trained in psychoanalysis as well as other psychotherapeutic approaches and, very importantly, also in the appropriate use of psychiatric medication. Most importantly, Dr. Zal prescribes psychiatric medications not as a panacea to solve all of his client's problems, but as a tool for the client to help him or herself with the psychiatrist's guidance and assistance. In fact, this holistic approach to treatment of GAD is what makes Dr. Zal so helpful and so successful in treating his anxious clients.

It is because of this holistic approach that I am so pleased that Dr. Zal asked me, an academic biological psychiatrist, to write this foreword. Dr. Zal's approach to treating his clients is exactly the approach that I have employed in my private practice. While I was heavily involved from the late 1950s on in controlled, academic research to find new antianxiety and antidepressant medications to improve my clients' suffering, I swiftly realized that medications, no matter how effective, were only tools to allow my clients to help themselves, preferably within the context of a warm psychotherapeutic counselor-client relationship.

Every client is a different individual and that is the way Dr. Zal approaches the treatment of all his clients. It is also quite clear to the reader that taking a good and extensive psychiatric and medical history is the foundation of any good treatment approach. Here we see Dr. Zal's success with his clients. He allows them to take their time to share with him their innermost thoughts. If I would be in need of a psychiatrist, Dr. Zal would be my choice.

Throughout the book, Dr. Zal espouses a realistic approach in helping his clients. He stresses the point that GAD is a chronic biological illness that has a genetic vulnerability and runs in families. At times of stress, it can escalate. Dr. Zal explains many of the common personality traits that anxious people often have, and I particularly like his concept of seeking contentment and not just happiness. He shows us that anxiety and worry can be handled and reduced, and he teaches his anxious clients which approaches are best for them to decrease their anxiety and become more functional and productive in their lives.

I have known Dr. Zal since the late 1970s, and over a period of ten years we conducted joint research in the pharmacological treatment of anxiety and depression. I have followed his professional career ever since. Dr. Zal has published three prior books in the field of mental health, including

Panic Disorder: The Great Pretender. Dr. Zal has assumed leadership roles in Philadelphia psychiatry, is a much respected lecturer, medical writer and editor on mental health topics and, most importantly, is one of the most outstanding clinicians I have ever known.

—Karl Rickels, MD
Stuart and Emily B. H. Mudd Professor of Psychiatry, University of Pennsylvania
Founder, University of Pennsylvania Private Practice Research Group

Introduction

Forty million adults suffer from anxiety disorders in the United States today. Of this, 6.8 million people have generalized anxiety disorder (GAD), which is our most common mental health problem. GAD is an inherited biological illness that may run in families. It is second only to major depressive disorder in lifetime frequency. Chronic anxiety can be demoralizing, limit your life and interfere with your ability to function. It may grow worse when you are under stress. Its clinical manifestations have great social, medical and economic consequences (most of the costs result from reduced or lost productivity).

Søren Kierkegaard, the founder of existentialism, first described anxiety in his 1844 book, *The Concept of Anxiety*. He believed that the freedom to choose without guarantees about the correct choice caused dread and anxiety.[1] His colleagues Karl Jaspers, Martin Heidegger and Jean-Paul Sartre also agreed that man's freedom to make choices is the source of his anxiety.[2] Jacob Mendes Da Costa noted the frequent association between chest pain and anxiety in soldiers who were upset by their experiences in the American Civil War.[3] His article, "On Irritable Heart...," published in 1871 in the *American Journal of Medical Sciences*, highlighted this connection. During the next hundred years, anxiety had a number of aliases, underlying the cardiac manifestations of anxiety. These labels changed after each major war. Cardiac Neurosis (Da Costa's Syndrome) became "neurasthenia" during World War I. World War II brought the term "anxiety state."

Sigmund Freud stripped away the emphasis on physical symptoms to lay bare a theoretical skeleton emphasizing emotional components. He saw anxiety as one of the keys to understanding human dynamics and coined the phrase "anxiety neurosis."[4] Psychoanalysis sees anxiety as a signal that certain unacceptable impulses (sexual or aggressive feelings) are trying to escape the unconscious and are trying to break into consciousness. Mental pain serves as a signal to mobilize other defense mechanisms to try and keep this material out of awareness. These unacceptable urges can be real or symbolic.[5]

A more modern view concentrates on the biological causes of anxiety. It involves three neurotransmitters, or hormone substances, that cause a nerve impulse to move from one nerve cell to another. They are gamma-aminobutyric acid (GABA), serotonin and norepinephrine. Particular emphasis is placed on the GABA system not working properly. GABA acts as an internally produced tranquilizer that decreases anxiety. People with GAD may have low levels of this naturally produced hormone.

Positron emission tomography (PET scan), which examines chemical changes in brain tissue, has shown that the neurotransmitters serotonin and norepinephrine also play a role in anxiety regulation. The discovery that these three hormones, or neurotransmitter systems, are involved in anxiety disorders allows us to recognize them as real biological conditions and true medical illnesses.

Anxiety is a universal feeling. To a moderate degree, anxiety has various positive aspects and can be considered "normal." It can serve as a biological warning system that is activated during times of potential danger or threat. It can prepare a person for an exam, speech or battle. It can increase alertness and effort and enhance your performance. It is the rapid beating of your heart as you await big news. It is the restless tension that you feel prior to taking a test or giving a business presentation. It is the worry that a parent experiences listening for a teenager to return home after their first solo car drive. It is the feeling of impending doom inherent in answering the boss's call. It can be conducive to learning and growth.

If these feelings become free-floating and increase in frequency and intensity, you have crossed the line from "normal" to "abnormal" anxiety. "Abnormal," or nonadaptive, anxiety is more severe, interferes with functioning and with your capacity to experience satisfaction or pleasure. These more persistent levels of anxiety can cause disorganization, impair concentration, create uncomfortable physical symptoms, disturb sleep and precipitate depression and fatigue.

At our first meeting I usually recognize anxiety clients because very often they come early for their appointments. Once they are seated in the treatment room, their tension flows across my desk in waves. By the end of the session, I am feeling their stress.

"Have you generally been nervous all of your adult life?" is one of the key questions that I ask if I suspect that I am dealing with an anxious person and I want to quickly narrow the diagnostic field and rule in GAD. Besides free-floating anxiety, nervous people show three other cardinal features: avoidance behavior, excessive unrealistic worry and vague physical complaints. Anxious people often also complain of fatigue, headache, insomnia and abdominal or chest pain. The degree of disability may vary. The course is chronic and variable. Symptoms often intensify during times of stress.

THE TRIAD OF ANXIETY

WORRY

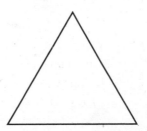

AVOIDANCE BEHAVIOR　　　PHYSICAL COMPLAINTS

The three features shown above, along with free-floating anxiety, are the cardinal characteristics of GAD. It is the most common of the anxiety disorders. To be diagnosed with this problem you must suffer from excessive anxiety and worry for at least six months in reference to a number of issues. The worry is difficult to control. The symptoms cause significant distress or impairment of functioning. The complaints are not due to the use of a substance, medical condition or other psychiatric disorder. You must show at least three other emotional or physical signs and symptoms of anxiety. These symptoms often result in significant emotional pain and prevent you from relaxing and enjoying life. Your anxiety can show in many ways:

Emotional Aspects of Anxiety

Feeling tense, keyed up or restless
Irritability
Apprehension
Excessive worrying
Feeling suddenly scared for no reason
Fear of heights, darkness or being alone
Social fears
Sexual worries
Fear of death or having a serious disease
Feeling panicky
Derealization (out of body experience)
Fear of losing control or going crazy
Feeling that something terrible is going to happen

Physical Aspects of Anxiety

CARDIOVASCULAR
Palpitations
Dizziness
Faintness or lightheadedness
Chest pain or pressure

RESPIRATORY
Shortness of breath
Hyperventilation
Choking sensation or lump in the throat

MUSCULAR
Muscle tension
Easy fatigability
Trembling/shaking
Weakness
Rubbery or "jelly legs"

GASTROINTESTINAL
Dry mouth
Indigestion
Nausea and vomiting
Butterflies in stomach
Diarrhea
Flatulence

OTHER
Sweating/hot flashes or chills
Headache
Constant urge to urinate
Numbness or tingling sensation
Spells of increased sensitivity to sound, light or touch
Difficulty in concentration/mind goes blank
Sleep disturbance
Exaggerated startle response
Skin disorders

Your physician or psychiatrist needs to rule out other emotional and physical disorders and rule in other overlapping, or *comorbid*, conditions. Individuals with a normal reaction to stress, major depression, personality disorders or those withdrawing from substance abuse or dependency can show anxiety. Anxiety can also be seen in acute psychosis and schizophrenia. People suffering from hyperthyroidism, hypertension, cardiac arrhythmias or mitral valve prolapse can all come in the door complaining of anxiety. Various medical disorders such as irritable bowel syndrome, asthma/chronic obstructive pulmonary disease (COPD) and pheochromocytoma, a hormone-producing tumor, can overlap with anxiety symptoms.

Generalized anxiety disorder clients may also suffer from other anxiety disorders such as obsessive-compulsive disorder (OCD), social phobia, post-traumatic stress disorder (PTSD) and panic disorder. Your doctor initially needs to decide if your complaints are emotional, physical or both. To decide this, we need to take a good health history, check all of your medications, question you about drug use or abuse and look at basic bloodwork. I usually ask for at least a complete blood count (CBC and Differential), comprehensive metabolic panel and thyroid profile (thyroid stimulating hormone [TSH], T3, T4). Therapists often may have to talk to your current and previous physicians. If you are diabetic, we may need to follow your glucose and HbA1C numbers. Fluctuations in your sugar levels can affect your mood. At times, a testosterone level may be helpful in men to differentiate between low energy due to anxiety and physical issues. Being given a specific diagnosis can give relief and even reassurance to some people. As they exhale, they often say, "You mean that all I have is anxiety? I thought that I was going crazy."

Anxiety is possible throughout the life cycle. It can hide within shy, inhibited children and adolescents in crisis. It can appear in young adults expanding their social and vocational options and can accompany the shattered expectations of midlife. GAD may actually be the prevalent mental disorder in the elderly. It is sometimes difficult to diagnose in this age group. Their bodily complaints and sleep problems can signify anxiety. Depression, dementia and even substance abuse can mask and/or produce anxiety symptoms. Primary medical problems as well as medication can also cause their anxiety. Studies have shown that GAD (affecting 7 percent of seniors) is more common in the elderly than depression, which affects about 3 percent of seniors.[6]

GAD is common, chronic and disabling. It is a real biological illness that is treatable. It is not a form of hypochondria or a sign of weakness. It usually presents with the four cardinal features noted earlier but can often present with physical complaints alone. Treatment options include education and reassurance, psychotherapy, cognitive-behavioral therapy (CBT), pharmacology, relaxation/meditation/biofeedback, exercise and diet. Spirituality is helpful to many. You must conquer the cycle of fear and reduce cognitive distortion. Thoughts such as "something terrible is going to happen" and "I am going to lose control" can escalate anxiety and fear. Try to interpret these feelings to simply mean "I am feeling nervous."

Managed care has marginalized many psychiatrists into just doing medication management. One of the biggest and most important changes during my long psychiatric career is the growth in the field of psychopharmacology and the benefits of psychiatric medication. However, there is no "magic pill" to solve all of your emotional problems. Psychiatric training is now moving toward a return to teaching residents and fellows to conduct therapy.

This book was written from my vantage point as a clinician working with real people. I provide both therapy and medication management. I feel that they are both important in obtaining relief from emotional distress. I take an eclectic but old-fashioned approach and offer individualized treatment suggestions that put the emphasis on the whole person. I will discuss conventional as well as alternative therapies. Many options will be offered.

Unlike many books that promise a cure, this one will present a more realistic picture of what treatment can accomplish for you. An appropriate expectation of psychiatric treatment is that it can offer education, reassurance, symptom reduction and control, teach coping mechanisms and ways to feel more in control, foster perspective and insight about the past and present and encourage growth and maturity. A positive therapist-client relationship is a strong therapeutic tool. A connection with your therapist can allow you to feel secure while you are learning to deal with your anxiety.

Therapy can help you understand yourself better and often can give you the support, encouragement and acceptance that you did not receive when you were young. Your parents may not have been able to give you everything you wanted emotionally, because their own parents may have been limited. Therapy cannot totally make up for the things that you did not obtain in childhood. It cannot completely fill or reverse the void often left by earlier unfulfilled needs for love or nurturing. However, if we can get you to feel better about yourself, reinforce your gains and offer support when needed, it goes a long way toward balancing the deficit.

However, psychiatric treatment cannot make you immune to anxiety. GAD is a chronic, lifelong condition that can wax and wane depending on your life stress. It is impossible to place a time limit on the appearance or disappearance of symptoms or when they will increase or decrease. The truth of the matter is that people who are anxious, even with good treatment, will not always be anxiety free. They can feel less anxious, feel anxious less often and be better able to cope with their nervousness when it does occur. But as I've said, anxiety is inherited: it is part of your DNA. Under certain circumstances and in certain situations, it may always pop up in your life. However, you can be less anxious more often and handle your anxiety better when it does arise. I will emphasize acceptance and proactive behavior rather than eradication, which is impossible.

There are many things that people can do to help themselves. Educating yourself about anxiety can be a first step in allowing perspective, reducing your feelings of apprehension and helplessness and allowing you to feel more hopeful and more in control of frightening feelings. This book is intended to help you understand stress and anxiety and to familiarize you with the symptoms of GAD and a broad range of possible treatment options. When you find yourself feeling apprehensive, tense and irritable, try the ten self-help techniques in this book that have proven beneficial to a wide variety of people suffering from anxiety. Hopefully, they will help you reduce your own anxiety, relax and enjoy life.

A GAD Case History: Paul's Story

"My anxiety is such a gut wrenching, horrible, terrified and scared feeling. It is a feeling of fear—I become a prisoner—scared to make a move—afraid that something bad will happen. I cannot sleep. At one point, I lost weight to the point that I had to drink extra liquid supplements. I feel a constant battle in my head. I get to a point that I just do not care what is wrong or right. I worry that I will never see the light and I will always be in the dark. It brings me to a point that I just want to run and never be found. It took me to such a low feeling that I could not go even one day without tears. I felt like I was in the bowels of hell. I cried unstoppably in the shower. I wound up on my knees just crying and feeling below nothing. I could go on but really didn't want to. There is so much more."

In spite of his gray hair, Paul appeared much younger than his fifty-eight years. He scrunched himself into the curve of the chair, looking timid and vulnerable. He never smiled; instead, he looked scared and apprehensive. Every time I asked him a question that made him feel uncomfortable or he shared a childhood trauma or a negative feeling, he nervously and continuously pulled on the hairs on his arm and rubbed the skin on his forehead. Whenever I felt that we had a particularly good talk where he shared significant material and had an insight, he would get up from his chair and say, "I guess this was a bad session."

Paul had obsessive-compulsive overlap symptoms. He needed to double- and triple-check things. For instance, if he didn't verify that the door of his house was locked when he left, he would become quite anxious. If his wife said that she had locked the door, he doubted it and had to go back and check. He liked things in order. "It gives me a sense of peace," he said. He sought symmetry. If pictures on the wall were not straight, he had to get up and fix them. He would say, "The purpose of the picture is to be straight." Paul could also be fidgety, had difficult falling asleep due to "thinking, thinking, thinking" and could become short of breath and hyperventilate when he was "nervous."

It took Paul more than ten years to pick up the phone, call a psychiatrist and come for help. He was treated on an outpatient basis for depression for more than twenty-five years by two different psychiatrists. He could become tearful, angry and anxious. He was prescribed various psychiatric medications. On one occasion, he got so upset that he felt he could not function. He was hospitalized at a local psychiatric facility. Six months after his second psychiatrist retired, he called me for an appointment. Initially, he seemed like a GAD client. He had the classic triad of anxiety, worry and avoidance as well as a family history of emotional problems (his mother had a "nervous disorder"). However, he had not told his prior psychiatrists or myself the whole story. It took him many sessions until he shared his secret with me.

His parents were in their forties when he was born. His sister was fifteen years older and out of the house by the time he was six. Both parents worked, so he was raised by his grandmother. He spoke about never having a childhood and never getting to do anything with his parents. He played ball and hung out but doesn't have many happy memories of his early days. When Paul was sixteen, his grandmother bled to death accidentally when she tried to cut a bandage off her leg. He vividly described his memory of the paramedics putting her in a rubber bag and his father rolling up the rug that was saturated with blood. "I still hear the zipper in my mind and see her in the bag," he said.

His secret took place between the ages of ten and twelve. With much hesitation, he finally related that during this time he had been sexually abused. At first it was by some older kids in his neighborhood, like the eighteen-year-old who seduced him into taking off his clothes because he wanted to see if his new camera worked. When Paul was fourteen, a man in his thirties befriended him and also sexually abused him. Paul still had bad dreams and flashbacks of these incidents and had trouble watching related news on television. "It makes me sick to think about it," he said. "They stole my childhood. I feel that I have a scarlet letter. I feel subhuman. Even when I go to confession, I do not feel clean. I feel dirty. I didn't say no. I was scared and wanted to please them. I thought that they would hurt me. It caused me anger and rage."

These experiences left him fearful and timid all his life. He felt that he had to take extra precautions to be safe. He worried constantly and felt like an inadequate failure. He never told anyone about the abuse because he was embarrassed, guilty and shamed, all strong emotions that can be painful.

In spite of these traumas and the energy he used carrying around his secret for so long, he still graduated from high school and worked for many years at a steel company. He has three children from his first marriage, which lasted ten years, and has been happily married to his second wife for eleven years. Between Paul and his wife, they have eleven grandchildren. Paul still works a few hours each day in a small store, doing paperwork.

Paul's Opinion of What Helped His Anxiety

"Therapy helped me. It made me look at things from a different perspective. I wasn't always receptive but what you said gradually sunk in and helped me. The medications...were like wonder drugs. They have helped make things better. [They]...took away my negative thoughts and tearfulness. I stopped lying in the bathtub in despair. [They]...took away my edginess and [helped] me relax and not be as jittery. My religion and my spiritual life are very important to me. The Church has been very supportive. I go to Mass every day. I place a lot of faith in God and his always being there for me. No matter what religion you practice, if you pray he will answer you. You will not always get what you want but you will get what you need. Exercise is also helpful. I walk three to four miles a day. I'm constantly running and hiking. Being outdoors takes me out of my state of mind. I feel like I'm free and no longer a prisoner."

My Opinion of What Helped Paul's Anxiety

In therapy, we dealt with Paul's feelings of guilt and shame. They initially came to the fore in discussing the situation when he took care of his mother, who had developed Alzheimer's disease. She was very irritable and uncooperative. He felt upset, because on occasion he lost his patience and yelled at her. He had never spoken to anyone who took care of a relative with Alzheimer's and did not know how difficult and frustrating that could be. He wasn't aware that there is no one right way to provide care for an elderly parent and that his negative feelings were not unusual in this stressful situation. He did not realize that you can still love a person although you are angry at his or her behavior. I had him read *The 36-Hour Day: A Family Guide to Caring for Persons with Alzheimer Disease.*[1] This was helpful. He commented, "I missed all the warning signs—the anger, the yelling, that I needed help."

His feelings of shame, embarrassment and guilt that he still had about the sexual abuse were more difficult to dissipate. They were intertwined with his sense of identity. Somehow, he believed that these acts had branded him as a homosexual. Even at age fifty-eight, he was fearful that a gay man would try to seduce him, so he felt that he constantly needed to be on guard. In some way, in spite of his heterosexual orientation and lifestyle, he felt that he could still be a sexual victim. He was surprised to learn that those young boys who abused him were not necessarily gay; they were just experimenting sexually and wanted to feel powerful. I also explained to him that being gay had to do with your adult sexual preference and not how you walked or talked. I told him that I doubted that a gay male would pick on a heterosexual older man. We also talked about pedophilia. The two older men who abused him were pedophiles and not homosexuals. He did not know this. I showed him a wonderful *Newsweek* article written by movie producer Tyler Perry. In the piece Perry revealed that he also had been molested as a youth. He wrote the column to a young boy involved in the Penn State scandal to tell him that he wasn't a victim—he was a survivor.[2]

To help Paul dissipate his considerable feelings of anger, I asked him to write a letter to the last man who sexually abused him. The following is some of what he wrote:

"I still remember and despise what you did to me after all these years. I remember the way that you lured me away from my friends. I still see the images in my head. It's too painful for me to write down what you did to me. It sickens me. I still feel you, hear you and see you in my mind. You started something in my life that I thought was good and it wasn't. What you did to me years ago is so disgusting and terrible, it still haunts me today. The actions performed by you on me and me on you make me sick. It has left me with years and years of memories that will never leave my mind. Now in this day and age of full media exposure, it seems to get worse.

"I can never, ever forget. The visual thoughts are haunting. I guess I cannot blame it all on you, because I am told that I may have been searching for something. But still, you were older than me. I despise what happened to me and think your actions were deplorable. I hate every thought of it. I hate every action that was done. Do I hate you?—no, I don't—But I hate the sins of our past. Years ago, I was filled with rage, anger and fear, and sometimes I still am. Trust me, the memories will never stop. The emotional roller coaster never slows down or has an end. I share this with no one. It is my hell. The side effects never stop. It cost me plenty of tears, fear and anxiety, as well as feeling useless and hopeless. It's a journey without an end."

Paul was locked into his routine because it helped him feel more secure. It was difficult to get him to try something new and take a risk which he thought was dangerous. I asked him to try an exercise which I call "follow your nose." I asked him to take a four-hour block of time, perhaps on the weekend when he was free, and do whatever he wanted. It sounds easy but can be hard for anxious people like Paul. He struggled with this concept. However, one day, he finally tried taking a walk in a different part of his favorite park. He actually enjoyed it.

Paul showed gradual improvement. It was difficult to quantify but there was a change. He looked more relaxed. He wasn't pulling on his hair and rubbing his face as much and his nightmares and flashbacks were far less frequent. He seemed happier and talked more in therapy. He started to have more realistic expectations of himself and others, while focusing on his positive attributes. He tried to allow himself to be less perfect and less "scrupulous." Although he was fearful, worried and hesitant, he tried new things and widened his "safe zone." Before our sessions, he was afraid to go anywhere new, but he eventually visited his son in New England and took a trip to California with his wife to visit her children.

Before, his trips away from home were limited mostly to a theme park. He called this "my ultimate safe zone—a place to relax and have fun. I don't have any scary dreams when I am there. I just feel free. I joke around and laugh with the kids." I suggested to him that perhaps this was the one place that he allowed himself to lighten up, be juvenile and compensate for his lost childhood. I tried to get across to him that he could give himself permission to relax and enjoy life like he did in the theme park in other situations as well. At first, he complained that doing more would be out of his comfort zone and bring him into the unknown, which he found scary. However, he then came up with the phrase "experiment with life" and seemed more comfortable and less threatened by this way of describing his dilemma. He agreed that he would try to experiment more and his wife later said that he was doing so.

Medication helped Paul. He was most recently on an antidepressant. Perspective has helped. Education has helped. Exercising and a religious connection have helped. In an effort to have him share his story of abuse with someone other than myself, I asked him to speak with his priest and see what response he got. He agreed to do this. I hoped that the priest would further reduce Paul's feelings of guilt, anxiety and shame.

Paul's vignette illustrates some of the pain anxious people experience. It also highlights various treatment modalities. Next, we'll look at steps to take and stories of several other special yet representative people as they share the anxiety in their lives with you. I will suggest possible solutions that they and I have used to relieve their anxiety, help them refocus, relax and enjoy life.

Part I

Steps to Relieve Anxiety

Chapter 1

Step 1:
Stop

Stop the world and the anxiety process for a moment. Give yourself time to recoup. Slow down and gain perspective. There is no danger. You don't have to race so fast. Perhaps you are putting yourself under time pressure. Give yourself permission to relax. Don't let the symptoms of anxiety control you. You can take charge of them.

People who are anxious move too fast physically and mentally. They always seem to be busy. Some experience physical symptoms such as heart palpitations and shortness of breath. Sometimes they are not even aware that they are feeling anxious and just feel pressured, tense and irritable. They may act restless and fidget if sitting too long. Often they feel compelled to do things like they were a wound-up clock. Overly perfectionist, they have a determination to get it right and have an exaggerated sense of what they and you "should be doing" and the specific way that tasks "should be done." They have to do them all on their own, in their own way, and often do not like how others complete a task, yet they complain that they have to do everything themselves. They often have a strong need to please others and therefore have trouble saying no. This puts them under further time pressure and increases their tension. They have difficulty unwinding and relaxing when they should be relaxing. Their to-do list grows longer and longer. By the end of the day they are tired, wiped out and unable to sleep. These behaviors make them more prone to burnout. Judy, one of my clients, has these problems.

Judy's Story

"My anxiety is my best friend. I guess my anxiety has been with me so long I became inexplicably comfortable with it. I was described as a 'hyper' child (although I did well in school), who never wanted to sleep. I think I must have thought that if I relaxed I would lose my energy level. My mother was the same way. She would clean, clean, clean and work, work, work. At one point, I was working full time, dating and going to graduate school. I had so many people I didn't want to disappoint. I was under stress and the anxiety returned big time. My coworkers described me as a 'hyper nut.' (In a good way!) I think that my anxiety worked for me. I could pull all-nighters and study and then go to work the next day. The anxiety or the 'hyper personality' became part of me. I lived with it, accepting that 'this is me.' I seemed to thrive on pressure but hated it at the same time. Although I did very well, I couldn't calm down when I wanted to. There were ebbs and flows; some years were worse than others. I am my mother's daughter."

Judy bounded into the office and onto a chair. She was forty-three years old. She carried a large red purse that caused her to be somewhat off balance. She talked with her whole body and threw herself into different positions like a rag doll. Judy complained of anxiety, palpitations, sweating, tension headaches, shortness of breath and feeling hot or cold. "Everything is overkill with me. I'm over the top," she said. Indeed, she did not seem to relax for a minute. My first thought was, *Where do I start with this lady?*

During the opening session, I took a psychiatric and medical history (a habit I always practice), asked Judy about her family, her education and her job history. I did a mental status examination which confirmed my initial impression that she was suffering from generalized anxiety disorder (GAD). At the end of the hour I said to her, "Judy, I had a job to do today. I had to make a diagnosis and formulate a treatment plan. Now, I have to ask you two things. Did you feel comfortable talking to me today? Did everything that I said to you seem to be relevant to you as a person or did you feel that I was trying to put you into a square hole in which you did not belong?" She answered that she had felt comfortable and that she felt that everything that I had said to her was about her and resonated with her. I stood up, smiled and shook her hand. "Then we have made a start."

Judy was not wrong in her assumption that she had inherited her anxiety from her mother. Research studies on twins have long hinted that anxiety-related personality traits such as worry, harm avoidance, tension, fear of uncertainty, fatigability and pessimism are 40 to 60 percent inherited. Human genetic studies have proven this premise to be true.[1] In 1996, *Science Magazine* reported evidence of a gene (the functional unit of inheritance) linked to individuals prone to these anxiety traits.[2] According to Gregor Mendel's genetic model of inheritance, two alternative forms of a gene, which carry a delivery system for the brain chemical serotonin, influence human "neuroticism" (anxiety and associated traits). One form results in more protein, more serotonin uptake and more neurotic behavior. The second form results in less protein, less serotonin uptake and fewer neurotic symptoms. An offspring exhibits one or the other of the genes but not a mixture of the two.[3]

It soon became apparent that Judy definitely also had issues concerning time pressure that added to her tension and stress. She told me that her father was in a long-term care facility and frequently needed to be hospitalized due to falls. In spite of having two sisters, she was the designated caregiver and took care of most of his needs. Her son had dropped out of college, lived at home and was not working. Her live-in boyfriend, although she said that he was emotionally supportive, didn't seem to do much around the house and was not always there physically or emotionally. She demanded an intense level of performance from herself, at work and everywhere else. These demands meant that she had no time for herself to unwind and relax. She constantly had too much to do and too little control over the time and manner in which things were done. This was aggravated by her inability to establish boundaries between her work and personal life.

Many times during our sessions, I said to myself, *I wish that I could just get Judy to learn to relax for a moment.* I tried to teach her a breathing exercise to slow her down and allow her to calm down. I illustrated the exercise myself. I took in a deep breath through my nose and let it out very slowly. I placed my hands flat on the top of my chest and moved them down slowly as I exhaled through pursed lips. This took me about fifteen seconds. I asked Judy to try it. She did it in two seconds flat as if she was blowing out birthday candles. I said, "Try it again and do it more slowly." By the fourth try, she had it up to eight seconds.

Judy often complained of feeling that she was going from one pressure cooker at work into another pressure cooker at home. I asked her to pause for a moment and allow her rational brain to seek a solution rather than responding with anxiety and irritability while under stress. I suggested that she try to think of a way that she could unwind and reduce her tension between the time that she left work and returned home. She answered, "Another therapist taught me a trick to help me stop bringing my job home. He suggested that when I leave work that I stand outside for at least ten seconds and tell my mind, 'work is over, no more thinking about it.' This is harder than it sounds. However, with practice, it works." I suggested she do the same thing before she entered her home, which she agreed was a good idea.

As I have gotten to know people who are anxious, I have noticed that there are certain themes that continually crop up in our conversations during therapy. Like many anxiety-prone people, Judy was also a perfectionist with high expectations of herself and others. Anything less than 100 percent was seen as failure. This is one reason that she hesitated to delegate some of her father's care to her sisters, because "They don't do it right."

She valued control and predictability. Any loss or threatened loss of control made her feel helpless and subsequently anxious. She had a need for too much control to feel secure and calm. Like other anxious people, she was overly concerned with what "should be." She felt that there was only one "correct" way to do things. She tended to see things as either black or white. This also made her more prone to anxiety. She would often say, "They should have done it this way." I would counter by saying "According to whom?" She would laugh because she saw my point. The word "should" reflected her need to do things according to her rule book. These rules allowed her to feel more in control but restricted her flexibility and spontaneity.

During one session, Judy went on and on about her mother. She spoke about how her mother had been hard on her and was big on guilt: "She was the disciplinarian in the family and beat the crap out of me. She was very hard to please. She felt that her increased anxious energy was productive but she felt that mine was non-productive. Mom worked all the time and was not there for me. She had a high-pressure job. Like me, she thrived under the pressure but hated it at the same time. I remember saying to her, 'This is a new generation, mom. I will never do all you do.'"

At this point, I asked her, "Did you like it when your mom acted that way?"

She answered with a loud and emphatic, "No!"

"Then why do you act that way toward *your* family members?" I asked. I could see the light bulb go on in her head.

She went on to talk about her sisters: "My twin sisters were born when I was two. When my parents brought the baby girls home from the hospital and I saw them for the first time, they told me that I took a bag of oranges and threw them one at a time at the two of them. I don't know how mom did it. She had to learn to cook, find a babysitter for my two younger sisters and me in the summer and maintain the house. Mom pushed me off to my grandmother, who died when I was twelve years old. My aunts were there for me, but basically I was alone. My father worked full time and belonged to a lot of organizations. He came home at six and expected dinner on the table. He spent time with us only on the weekends."

Judy's Opinion of What Helped Her Anxiety

"My mother dropped dead at sixty-eight years old (burst an artery in her brainstem). Stress kills! That's when I went to therapy for the first time. The rug had been yanked from beneath me. My rock was gone. Dr. Zal is the third therapist I have had. He does 'talk therapy.' Sometimes you just can't see yourself and need that outside professional opinion to point things out to you. He can zero in on what I call my 'bad behaviors' in dealing with anxiety. He is honest and direct. He calls me on my crap, as I call it. We are getting to the root of my anxiety. He is helping me deal with the stress caused by taking care of my dad, who is in a long-term care facility. He is teaching me how to say no! I have trouble saying no to anyone who asks me to do something for them (even people I don't consider close to me) and it just adds to my stress. I get upset if people don't like me. He helps me by asking easy questions such as, 'Do you like everyone?' I answer, 'Of course not.' He adds, 'Then why does everyone have to like you?' His query stops me dead in my tracks.

"I used to handle stress by eating poorly, drinking too much coffee, smoking more. It didn't work. I still felt increased pressure, felt overwhelmed and couldn't get things done. I had trouble concentrating and making decisions. I worried constantly. I had 'stress eczema,' headaches, insomnia and muscle tension and spasms. In therapy, we have discussed better ways to handle stress. I have learned new coping skills. I am exercising more, have decreased my caffeine and take time to sit down and eat right. I do meditation and yoga. If I can't sleep, I get up and do something constructive until I feel tired again. I try to not define my value in life only through my job. I try to enrich my life outside of work by spending more time with my friends, family and boyfriend. (We have a 'date night' now every month, for just the two of us.) I try to do things that I like, even if I have to schedule time for fun. I like politics and writing. In fact, I'm a political junkie. I am trying to stop being 'superwoman.' I try to pace myself, organize my time and prioritize important activities. I try to be real about what I can and can't do. I have decided that I will not do any more overtime at work without being paid for it. I am letting my twin sisters help more with my dad. I am trying to stop worrying about the future so much! I am trying to enjoy today.

"Dr. Zal also gave me several anxiety-decreasing exercises, one of which is called 'deep breathing.' When he asked me in the office to take a slow, deep breath, he said, 'That was it? Not even close.' As simple as it sounds, it takes practice to do this exercise. I have to be constantly reminded that the push that I feel I receive from my anxiety is often a false assumption. I am so used to doing it the old way. So I practice every day. Every night, when I leave work and before I enter the house, I take time to 'de-stress.' Visualization techniques that I use are also helpful. I am soon to join Maum Meditation to further help my relaxation. I have a lot of work to do, but with Dr. Zal's guidance and some relief from the medication that he prescribed, I'll get there. I'm calmer, but I still freak out a little. I'm a work in progress but I am getting better."

My Opinion of What Helped Judy's Anxiety

Treatment for Judy included many aspects. Some of our goals were to help her relax, reduce her time pressures and allow her to feel better about herself. I educated her about her anxiety and gave her reassurance that she was not crazy. From the beginning, the positive therapeutic relationship between us allowed her to feel more secure and calmer. Initially, I fulfilled her unconscious need for an older therapist who was accepting and whom she felt would not hurt or punish her. Judy grew more tolerant of her anxiety as she understood her genetic propensity and realized that it wasn't her fault.

As you see above, we sometimes used modified cognitive therapy techniques to test out some of her assumptions, challenge her inaccurate thinking and give her perspective. Laughter helped. I often joked with her, which allowed her to relax. She was taught relaxation techniques including deep breathing and visualization. We discussed lifestyle changes, such as exercise, diet and reducing her caffeine intake. She brought yoga and meditation into the equation.

When Judy came to me, she was taking an antianxiety medication twice a day. I switched her to a different medication, because her original prescription only lasted four hours whereas my prescription lasted about eight hours.

In therapy, Judy mentioned that her mom was hard to please and was big on guilt. She worked all the time and was often not home. Judy grew up feeling that she was "bad" and thought that this behavior had caused her mom's actions. She felt that any female authority figure and sometimes the world would "beat the shit out of her." This made her feel fearful, angry and inadequate. She was also an "injustice collector" who always fought for the underdog. However, in spite of her childhood, Judy saw her mom as "her rock" and wanted to please her. She became tearful when I first pointed out this dynamic to her and why her verbally abusive female supervisor at work made her so angry and was such a problem for her. Unconsciously, she hoped that her next interaction with her supervisor would be better and that if she could just do her job more efficiently that it would help the process and finally get her the approval and positive feedback that she craved.

Judy described her father as "the best daddy ever. He was calm. He was not a disciplinarian and was always there for us. He took good care of us." He also made her feel safe in spite of a mother who "beat the crap out of me." This helps explain why she was so intense in trying to do everything she could to keep her father alive. It also explains why she chose three different older male therapists. I tried to instill in Judy a sense of self-worth, even if she didn't please everyone. She was smart, had a solid work ethic, was a good friend and really cared about people. I tried to help her to see that she was a capable, strong woman who had been standing on her own two feet since age twelve and had done well on her own. Perhaps she didn't need a constant safety net. Perhaps she didn't need a therapist cum father figure in her life to constantly support and protect her. As she gained these new perspectives, she started to realize that there was no danger in her life any longer. She started to give herself credit for being capable and realized that she was not the problem.

Judy's annoyance with her two sisters went back further than when her father entered the long term care facility. She realized that she was angry at her siblings, not only because they didn't do things her way, but also because she resented their intrusion into her life when she was a young child. When they were born, she lost her prime position in the household and she was given increased responsibility before she was ready. At first she was afraid to tell them that she was angry that they didn't do their share for their father.

She reluctantly took on the role of designated caregiver. Although she complained a lot, in some ways it fulfilled her needs, particularly to feel in control and therefore safe. As she started to understand these issues, she was better able to insist that her sisters share the workload.

After her twin sisters were born and her grandmother died, she noted, "I was alone." Judy felt that she needed outside support or she would be helpless, vulnerable and isolated. In her present life, she felt that she could not rely on her son. She was angry at his behavior and had no respect for him because he had dropped out of school and was not working. She could not rely on her boyfriend because, although he was emotionally supportive, he was not always around and "didn't always get it." Judy had grown up trying to please people so that they wouldn't leave her and would be there to protect her so she wouldn't feel bad or guilty. She had been in therapy with several different counselors for a long time because she felt that she needed this constant support.

Judy felt guilty about her son's life performance. He didn't fit the mold that she envisioned and was not a reflection of her way of dealing with the world. He was a child of divorce and she blamed herself for his adolescent behavior. During her therapy, he started working in the same facility where she was employed. He did well and she got positive feedback from her co-workers. This helped Judy feel better about herself as a mother and allowed her to understand that perhaps he did have some potential to be emotionally supportive to her in the future.

I encouraged Judy to spend more quality time with her boyfriend, which helped her feel loved, appreciated and more supported. He had not offered on his own before, because he felt that she did not have the time and was not interested. By being more proactive, she was starting to take charge of her anxiety by saying "Stop" to the anxiety process.

Chapter 2

Step 2:
Breathe

Take a deep breath. Draw air in through your nose and let it out very slowly through pursed lips. Take your time and don't rush the technique. This breathing exercise can be done one to three times in any situation. People will not even be aware that you are doing it. It will slow your pulse rate and help you calm down and relax.

The way we feel is affected by the way we breathe. When we are upset, we are often told to take a deep breath. But when we are feeling anxious or frightened, we don't just need to take a deep breath; we need to take a breath *and* exhale slowly. Breathing out, not breathing in, is associated with relaxation. Deep, slow, diaphragmatic breathing is a behavioral relaxation technique that can be taught to reduce or modify symptoms of anxiety. Watch a baby breathe. You will see its stomach—not just its chest—rise and then fall as the breath is released. Breathing retraining causes arousal reduction. Just as hyperventilation is taken by the nervous system as a sign that the body is under stress, deep diaphragmatic breathing sends a signal to the nervous system that "there is no danger—you can relax." When you are affected by a stressor, your body goes into the fight-or-flight response. One of the components of this response is an increase in your breathing rate and a move to upper-chest breathing. Diapragmatic breathing can reverse this process.

This simple exercise made a great difference in Matt's life. Let's look at how and why:

Matt's Story

"My anxiety is a battlefield. It has both a mental and a physical aspect. I worry and live with various fears on a daily basis. I get nervous when I am in an interview or meeting, a crowd of strangers, while driving (particularly if I am going somewhere new) or anywhere that I feel that I am trapped and can't escape easily. I feel overwhelmed. The negative thoughts pile up and seem insurmountable. When these feelings last for a while, I start to beat myself up for not being able to get it together and I become depressed. I also start thinking that I am getting physically sick, developing a new allergy or having a stroke. I think that I am losing my mind and will need to check into the asylum. I also get obsessive and start double-checking locks and the stove to see if it is on. My chest gets tight and there is pain on either side of my upper body. My back and neck become tight. My stomach churns. I get bouts of dizziness. I feel like adrenaline shocks are shooting through my body. I sigh a lot.

Sometimes, the physical symptoms can be much worse. I feel the tightness in my neck and back as well as the pain in my chest. As the anxiety grows, I begin to feel that I am not breathing right. I can't take a full breath. I can't swallow. Then my heart starts beating faster and I feel tightness and throbbing in my temples. As the anxiety increases and overwhelms me, I hit panic mode. My lips, the sides of my face, hands and feet will go numb and tingle. I feel like I have hive-like blotches on my face. Once my face was so numb and hot that I thought my eyes would be forced shut while driving and that I would crash. Immediately after the stressful situation passes, the numbness starts to go away but leaves my face and lips feeling puckered. I actually feel silly at that moment looking at myself like I just sucked on a lemon."

When I first met Matt, he was twenty-eight years old. He had had surgery for strabismus (being cross-eyed) and later a gastric bypass which brought his weight down from 430 to 230 pounds. Although his appearance was improved, it did not change his low self-esteem. He complained of feeling lonely. He had a college degree in fine arts and multi-media but in spite of being bright and creative, he only had a low-level technical job. Matt had a history of panic disorder; however, it was his generalized anxiety and low-grade chronic depression that brought him to my office for therapy. His anxiety was persistent, demoralizing and interfered with his functioning. For the most part, he had suffered in silence. The gastric surgery eight years prior had left him with multiple "stomach problems," including gas, nausea and constipation. He reported that he had been taking an antidepressant that inhibited the reuptake of serotonin and norepinephrine for four years and at top therapeutic dose. Each time that his family physician tried to lower the dose, Matt felt that it caused "pill withdrawal," upset his digestive system and threw his nervous system into turmoil, giving him increased anxiety, stomach pains and dizziness. He was adamant about not giving up his pills.

Matt was also convinced that many of his anxiety symptoms, particularly the numbness and the facial sensations and manifestations, had a physical cause. The presence of vague physical symptoms, often involving every system of the body, is an important feature of GAD. However, his ill-defined facial symptoms were unusual: they did not seem to be due to drug abuse, caffeine or medication. There was no family history of thyroid disease or diabetes. I was pleased when he told me that his family physician had also referred him to an endocrinologist for evaluation. A few weeks later, I received a report from the endocrinologist. He had ordered hormone studies to try to explain Matt's symptoms but was pessimistic that the results would give him an answer. He also wanted to rule out an allergic reaction. All the studies came back within normal range.

Matt's initial evaluation showed much "grist for the mill" for therapy. I decided to follow my gut reaction that his facial symptoms were due to anxiety. Education is a crucial part of the initial treatment process. Knowledge allows perspective, reduces feelings of helplessness and increases a sense of control over frightening symptoms. I decided to go back to basics and taught Matt to do a breathing exercise to see if that would help his symptoms. I told him to take in a deep breath through his nose and then let it out very slowly through pursed lips. Remember, it is the slow letting out of air that lowers the pulse rate and encourages relaxation. Most likely, Matt hyperventilated when he became anxious. This rapid breathing caused a decrease of carbon dioxide (CO_2), which upset the body's acid balance and caused physical symptoms such as muscle spasms and contractures. The deep breathing exercise helped bring this balance back to normal. The same effect can be gained by having the client breath into a paper bag, thus rebreathing CO_2. I hoped that this exercise would allow Matt to consider anxiety as a causative factor in his distress, offer him a new coping skill and help us form a therapeutic alliance.

Matt's biggest challenge was trying something new, particularly if it was geographically outside of his comfort zone. As with many anxiety-prone people, two of his stumbling blocks were his difficulty with change and his fear of the unknown. Change is difficult for anyone; for nervous people, because they value control and predictability, change is a haunted house filled with dark rooms. Any loss or threatened loss of control like a new job, a move to a new location, meeting new people or even trying new things causes them to feel helpless and subsequently anxious. They catastrophize and anticipate a negative outcome. It is difficult for them to relax and just go with the flow.

Anxious inner voices from the past often act as roadblocks to action for these individuals. When they are planning a trip, they may hear an internal voice saying, "That's awfully far from home." The inner voice may stem directly from parents, grandparents, teachers or older siblings who may have been anxious themselves and significantly influenced the clients' lives. Unfortunately, people who are anxious seem to accept these internal warnings as dictums rather than as a sign of the other person's own anxiety and fear. I try to help my clients step back from these warnings and consider their own desires and choices. I offer encouragement by saying, "Do you really need all that protection? You do not have to listen to the committee in your head. Think it through yourself and use your own judgment to decide what is right for you."

Matt faced a double problem: There was a history of anxiety on both sides of his family. He described his mother as intelligent, warm and affectionate but also overbearing, anxious and overprotective. She had multiple health issues and often stayed in bed for a week. "Pills and doctors—she had a fix for everything," Matt said. His maternal grandmother also got attention by complaining about physical things. His mother was the disciplinarian in his childhood home and often threatened him with a wooden spoon. His father, a draftsman, was "cold and unemotional but also anxious and a worrier." His father could be sarcastic and had a rule book about what was appropriate. He worried constantly about his father's reaction. At the beginning of therapy, I always ask clients to describe the people who raised them. Looking back at their descriptions often gives me clues to better understand how they became who they are and how they may see other people. Insight often comes from these connections.

These themes all played out in Matt's life. Anxiety, particularly about being away from home, had been an issue with him for some time. His dream growing up was to go to New York and become a musician. His mother told him, "Go to college. That's what I need from you." She told him to be "the best." Feeling great pressure, he went to a university in New York to study music technology. He became depressed and anxious and often couldn't stop crying. Feeling worthless, embarrassed and ashamed, he took a semester off, returned home and worked for a title company. Then he attended college in Philadelphia and majored in multi-media. He wrote music and recorded voiceovers. He still speaks of New York as "the scene of my failure."

Admitting that he needed to seek praise and approval his whole life, Matt was very sensitive to the remarks of others. "I didn't think I had done a good job unless someone told me." He easily felt rejected. He hated going to a private school with religious connections. He talked of how a teacher in seventh grade put him down and how he subsequently became depressed, had stomach problems and wet his bed. "She told us we were bad if we didn't do things perfectly," he said. His anxiety and stomach problems increased when he started a "real job" and kept him from doing things. He spoke of how his father and grandmother called him "a fat pig." Once, in his twenties, he dated someone who went to another church and he contemplated converting. His mother said, "You're giving up your family?" and made him feel guilty, thus putting an end to his religious exploration.

He started to understand how angry he'd been since childhood. He seldom said anything negative or stood up for himself or his thoughts due to his fear that others would not like or approve of him. By talking about his feelings in therapy, he realized that not everyone might be judgmental like his family. He realized that his childhood world was different from the larger outside world that he now inhabited. Gradually, he started to take risks and verbalize his feelings and desires more often outside of the therapy room. Although scared at first, he soon found that the results were positive and liberating.

Matt carried his insecurities and anxieties into his personal relationships. He was emotionally needy, had trust issues and could easily become jealous. He had had several significant relationships since age nineteen. Most recently, Matt had been dating David for several months, whom he described as intelligent, stable and mature. One of the main problems was that David lived one hundred miles from Matt's home. At first, David drove and they went out in the Philadelphia area. Gradually, as the relationship became more serious, there was pressure on Matt to visit David. There was also the issue of doing new things together, such as attending the theater, seeing family members and going to social functions. This meant driving on strange roads and to new places, which brought his anxieties to the forefront. He often used stomach pains or other physical complaints to avoid going.

Eventually Matt showed improvement with therapy. As he learned things about himself, he felt a little more confident and started taking more risks. He did better with change and the unknown and began to see how his anxiety and avoidance kept him from reaching his goals. At first, he would not drive alone and only drove to Harrisburg when David came to his house and went with him. Therapists call this using a "phobic partner." Finally, Matt took the chance and drove himself to Harrisburg, sometimes using side roads to avoid the expressway and turnpike. He slowly drove greater distances and tried more new things, much to David's pleasure.

Several months into therapy, he decided to see an Akashic healer, who told him about "The Book of Life" (a belief in universal memory and inter-connection) and taught him meditation. At first Matt told me about the healer as if I wouldn't approve. When I said that anything he did to help himself was okay with me and that really his healer and I were both trying to help him feel more in control but in different ways, he relaxed and became less defensive. He had found two people whom he respected and who accepted him unconditionally. He started to gain perspective in his relationship. He realized that David's need for "alone time" was not a sign of rejection. He started to ask for more responsibility at work and looked for new employment. With great trepidation, he went on several job interviews and obtained a much more significant position.

Matt's Opinion of What Helped His Anxiety

"With the help of Dr. Zal and spiritual practices, I have learned several methods to lessen my anxieties. The best tool for an acute anxiety attack is the breathing exercise. This alleviates the tightness and numbness in my face and hands (and gets rid of the blotches on my face) pretty quickly. It is hard to think of and practice in the moment of stress. But it works.

"I learned a lot about myself in therapy. I understand that I use health issues to feel more in control and avoid things that I am afraid to do. I also learned that part of my anxiety is created by holding back emotions. I used to use crying to release a lot of physical and mental symptoms (particularly feeling upset or angry). I fought crying for a long time as it is not considered "manly." It is not always appropriate in all situations, but if alone in a safe place, I say let it out. I have learned that my feelings can also be let out safely just by sharing them with someone I trust. I also try to use what I call 'The Zal Method' of dealing with my anxiety. I ask myself what anxiety or feeling is underlying my physical symptom. I don't always buy it but I at least give it a chance. Often, he is right and I think of something that I'm anxious or upset about. Now, I bulldoze through my worries. I can't waste my time.

"My antidepressant medication has been slowly reduced. I still will not give it up entirely. Perhaps it is my 'last parent' or security blanket. Perhaps it is my safety net that I can turn to in time of need. I am learning that I have been standing on my own two feet for a long time and doing quite well. Maybe I do not need a safety net.

"My involvement with Siddha Yoga practices has taught me how to meditate. Every morning, I spend at least ten minutes focusing my breathing and clearing my mind of all thoughts. It is tough to learn and does not happen instantly, but over time I have gotten to the point where I can clear my mind in five minutes and actually not feel anxiety for that time in meditation. I also feel it affects the stress level of the rest of my day in a positive way. My spiritual leader also taught me that 'We are all alone. God is inside us." This idea has helped me be less dependent on others.

"After taking a class from a Reiki Master, I learned to perform Reiki on myself. Reiki is the movement of spiritual energy or Qi through the body. It is meditative and whether it is a placebo effect or not, it aids in relieving my stress physically and mentally.

"Finally, one of the most important steps in lessening anxiety over time is positive self-talk. I consciously make an effort to recognize my accomplishments in fighting my anxiety and refuse to beat myself up if I fall short of my own expectations in the battle. I compare how I handled a situation in the present to how I would have handled it a year ago or two years ago and realize how far I have come. I recognize that there is no magic answer or instant fix, but each little step I take further into the battlefield is a win."

My Opinion of What Helped Matt's Anxiety

I have seen the simple breathing exercise calm people. However, some of Matt's physical symptoms of anxiety, particularly those involving his face, were far worse than average. I taught Matt the deep breathing exercise, hoping for the best. After two weeks he returned and told me that he drove a longer distance than usual and his anxiety grew progressively worse with each mile. His lips, the sides of his face and his hands and feet became numb and tingled. Hive-like blotches appeared on his face. He did the deep breathing exercise. After three tries, he looked in the car mirror and the blotches were gone. He was astonished. Seeing this technique work allowed him to have greater trust in therapy and my view of the nature and cause of his anxiety.

When I first saw Matt, I felt that, although he was unhappy, frustrated and had a history of depression, he was no longer clinically depressed. He had GAD and a history of panic disorder. Although his medication was an antidepressant, it was also helpful for insomnia and anxiety. Matt was not wrong when he said that he got increased anxiety, stomach pains and dizziness when he tried to get off his medication (which is known to have withdrawal symptoms). I suggested that we gradually decrease his dosage and place him on an antianxiety medication that would help his anxiety and prevent his panic attacks from returning. It took him five months to try this for the first time.

Matt incorporated yoga, meditation and other alternative therapies as well as spirituality into his treatment plan. He felt that his association with a spiritual leader was very helpful. This involvement allowed him to bring religion back into his life in a way with which he felt comfortable. It gave him something to hold on to during times of stress. He had come back to religion but in his own way.

In therapy we addressed many issues. Matt's mother and maternal grandmother were both role models who put much emphasis on physical problems and believed that a pill was the answer to everything, even though it sometimes isn't. This revelation moved Matt to allow me to slowly reduce his antidepressant medication. Matt internalized feelings of anger and guilt and denied his need for support and dependency. All of these issues got in the way in his new relationship with David. As time went by I was able to get him to verbalize these feelings. In any new relationship, we project our early wishes onto the other person just as the client projects them onto the therapist. As we get to know the person better, we start to see flaws and limitations. Gradually, Matt was better able to accept David, "warts and all."

Therapy helped Matt with his self-esteem and allowed him to feel better about himself. He had a distorted perception of himself, particularly his body image. Some of this was due to the message that he received in childhood that he was "a cross-eyed fat pig." I helped him reduce feelings of shame and guilt, stay away from self-pity and begin to like himself more. He started a diet. I also helped him see that he did not have to give others so much power over him. As Eleanor Roosevelt said, "No one can make you feel inferior without your consent."

To reduce his need for control and predictability, I pointed out that his life history showed no evidence of loss of control. There was no family history of psychosis. If anything, his problem was *too much* control. I tried to teach him that his personality probably would never allow him to lose complete control.

The most significant gain in therapy for Matt was his gradual willingness to travel greater distances, take risks and still feel in control. At first, he traveled to another city to see his lover and visit people in the area. Then, he took another job in a location that was outside of his comfort zone. Finally, with his dependency needs and anxiety in better focus, he was able to leave therapy and take an advanced position in a neighboring state. His anxiety battle had, at last, been partially won.

After several months had passed since I had last spoken to Matt, I called him to check his progress. He seemed happy and confident; his first words were, "I'm doing well. I just graduated from school with a master's degree in instructional technology. I gave my dissertation presentation in front of thirty people."

Matt told me that he was still working for the same firm: "It's been rough—a lot of management changes—but I stuck in there. I am doing consulting work on the side with a young firm. I'm handling stressful situations better. It's been good, especially with driving. You would be proud. I drive all over now, even across bridges. It's amazing. At first, I did it with my partner and then started to drive myself. Now I'm cruising on the highway. We are still together. If the fears do come up, I do the breathing exercise. I no longer need to be tethered to home. We will see how it goes from here. My anxiety is manageable. If it does present, I have the tools to handle it and it's just a bump in the road. Sometimes I just say to myself, what is the worst thing that can happen?"

What surprised me the most was what happened when I read him the first line of his vignette, where he compared his anxiety to a battlefield. Although he remembered writing the words, he could no longer relate to them because so much had changed in his life. I could see that he had come a long way from that insecure, upset and anxious young man whom I had met years ago. I was happy for him.

Chapter 3

Step 3: Refocus

Refocus. Concentrate on the here and now. Throw away those underlying negative feelings, particularly those from the past. Don't play the victim. Leave the past behind. Don't take it all so seriously. Give yourself permission to lighten up, smile and enjoy the moment. You are allowed to relax and have fun. All those bad things happened a long time ago. This is now. You are older, wiser and more in control.

Penny and Susan, two of my clients, are as different as night and day. However, they do share two things in common. They both have GAD and they both had an alcoholic parent who affected their lives and intensified their innate anxiety.

These women are not alone. Alcoholism statistics tell us that seventy-six million people in the United States alone have been exposed to alcohol dependency in the family. More than nine million children live with a parent dependent on alcohol.[1] Alcoholism is a disease involving the body, mind and spirit that often reflects psychological stress. This tension can spill over onto the children in the house, creating feelings of fear and insecurity. Children absorb anxiety like a sponge.

Gilda Berger calls alcoholism "the family disease" in her book, *Alcoholism and the Family*.[2] An alcoholic can create chaos, disrupt family life and cause harmful effects to all of its members that can last a lifetime. Children of alcoholics often show symptoms of anxiety and depression, feelings of shame, resentment, numbness, helplessness, lack of friends and problems with intimacy. They often live in fear and anticipation of danger. They have a low trust level due to a history of a sea of empty promises. Some have difficulties putting their painful childhood and adolescent memories behind them.

In families such as these, life revolves around the alcoholic. The other members unconsciously give up their own needs and take on roles that are helpful to the family unit in an effort to maintain peace and balance in their dysfunctional world. They can take on the role of caretaker, enabler, responsible one, family hero, cheerleader, mascot or lost child. As they grow older, the children of alcoholics often have trouble giving up these roles. As adults, both Penny and Susan compensated for feelings of inadequacy and helplessness by trying to appear strong. Their anxiety interfered with their enjoyment of life in the present. Both of them needed to learn to refocus, not get lost in the past and realize that they have grown physically and emotionally and have developed many new adult resources since they were entrenched in their threatening childhood world a long time ago.

Penny's Story

"My anxiety is the way that I avoid becoming the monster. I cannot relax. I'm so worried about what might happen next. I wish my mind could rest. I feel so keyed up. When something is upsetting me, I feel shaky inside. My breathing changes and my mind is not clear. The anxiety overtakes me. My heart feels like it skips a beat. I become short winded and have trouble catching my breath.

"I wake up anxious and afraid. I can't get enough air. When I make plans and am anticipating a good time at an event, anxiety makes me feel that it won't happen and even looking forward to something good becomes stressful. Then the negative 'what ifs' start. What if something bad happens? What if I lose control?"

Penny became my client when she was forty. She explained that she had a thirty-year history of psychiatric outpatient treatment for anxiety. In her late teens, she had a history of dependency on medications. She had not taken anything since. She was divorced and had three children. She had a good work history. Her alcoholic father had died of a heart attack ten years before. She still remembered his rage, his cursing and his angry voice. "When I think about it, I feel like my brain is throbbing," she said. She described her father as being outgoing and friendly to others when he was sober, but in the house, he was cold and distant. He often made promises that he didn't keep. "It was constant chaos," she said. "My father could easily blow up and be explosive. He once pulled a knife on me. He was physically abusive to my mother. He often hit me so hard that it left welts on my skin. I was so scared. I often hid under the table. I was always afraid of what would happen next. I had to prepare myself and protect myself. He was a monster."

She also told me that her paternal grandfather had molested her when she was four. She described her mother as a woman who was emotionally disconnected, depressed and fearful, shut away in the house and taking medication for her nerves. Penny worried about her mother and felt that she always had to look out for her and protect her from her father. It was an ambivalent relationship. "She always put me down," Penny said. "Nothing that I did was good enough. She once threatened to cut my fingers off if I didn't stop biting my nails." In spite of the fact that her mother used her as a confidante, she didn't feel that her mother loved her: "She would wake me up at night to go out and get pizza and beer for my father. I had weight issues. She would make me go to the tap room carrying the empty beer bottles for rebate. I felt embarrassed and degraded with all the men looking at me. I would retreat to my room. It was my sanctuary where I felt safe."

Penny was left with a lot of anger, lack of connection to others, depression and anxiety. "I have a need to look strong but I always feel lonely and have trust issues," she said. She constantly struggled with how to deal with her own angry feelings: "I feel a lot of anger sometimes to the point of lunacy and rage…I'm afraid I'll spaz out on the wrong person and tell them what

I think. I'm afraid I'll hurt someone physically. It's frightening even to me." Like many people who are anxious, she suppressed negative feelings and anger, because she was fearful that such feelings would cause a loss of control or disapproval from others. Because of their negative thought patterns, anxiety-prone people tend to be pessimistic. They ruminate, brood and stew. They tend to catastrophize and over-generalize. Their constant fretting clouds their perspective. They are sure that their negative reasoning reflects reality, that they are losers and will fail. This attitude often leads to depression.

Sometimes, Penny became depressed and withdrawn and showed physical symptoms, such as muscle spasms and headaches. She was very sensitive to criticism, yet she would occasionally lose her temper irrationally and push people away. She constantly struggled with wanting to be closer to her children, her boyfriend and her co-workers. However, she had problems with trust and maintaining closeness which interfered with her ability to do this. Her expectations were high and she quickly became frustrated if she felt that others did not respect her. It scared her when people lost their temper at work. Once when a woman screamed at Penny at her job, she said, "I'm afraid of people who talk like that. You never know what's going to happen. I saw abuse and violence when I was growing up. I can't deal with it. I have zero tolerance. I'm insecure."

Although she seemed to be making progress at times, Penny had difficulty maintaining it and things remained the same. Always feeling like the victim, she just could not seem to find a middle ground between her mother's and father's behavior. Either she was depressed, passive, withdrawn, avoidant and suffering from vague physical complaints or she was disappointed and angry at everyone. "I can get ugly," she said. "I scream and curse at my boyfriend. He is judgmental and critical like my parents. Once when we were in my car I got so angry at him that I hit the steering wheel so hard in a rage that I sprained my hand...I don't feel peaceful inside. I try one way and if that doesn't work, I try the other way. Something is missing. I always feel a big void. This big emptiness is always there. I feel that I'm not important to anyone." In between these two sets of behaviors was a constant feeling of anxiety and tension. "I feel afraid that I'm not going to be able to keep my head and maintain control.

I feel alone. I have no allies." At times, she felt like the vulnerable, powerless, ten-year-old child that she once had been.

Penny's Opinion of What Helped Her Anxiety

"I want the world to see me as strong. Some situations make me feel like when I was ten—emotionally threatened and helpless. I try to remember that I am not ten years old. I am not helpless any more. I try to distract myself and refocus. I take a deep breath and tell myself that I'm okay. I tense my muscles and then relax. No one can see me do this. I tense and relax again, while taking a deep breath and exhaling slowly. My heart rate and breathing will slow. I will feel a sensation of calm, mentally and physically. I relax and realize that I don't have to be either black or white. I don't have to be sweet or the monster. I don't have to retreat to my room to avoid things. I can just be me. My anxiety tells me that I am trying to avoid becoming the monster and trying to stay in control and not lose my temper. I am learning to deal with my resentment differently."

My Opinion of What Helped Penny's Anxiety

Penny was raised by two limited parents who both had anger issues. She particularly identified with her father's rage and was anxious that she would one day act like him. Identification is an unconscious mental process whereby an individual becomes like another person in one or several aspects. Your adaptive and defensive reaction patterns are often attributable to identification with either a loved or feared person. Freud would say that Penny identified with the aggressor (her father), whom she feared. In therapy, we deal with the fact that anger is a normal emotion; however, it is how we deal with it that defines us. When we share our anger, we also have to know with whom we are sharing. What is their level of emotional maturity? A mature person can react to your anger constructively. They may apologize and say something along the lines of "I'm sorry. I didn't know that that bothered you. I will try to deal with it differently next time." An emotionally immature person may turn it around, throw the anger back at you, blame you and point out your defects.

Viktor Frankl says that although you cannot control biology or genetics when it comes to resembling your parents, you can control your behavior.[3] Whenever Penny got into a situation that irritated her, she began to feel helpless like a ten-year-old again and her anger welled up. Most times, she became anxious as she tried to control her negative emotions. Sometimes she failed and, in her own words, she became like her father, "the monster." When all else failed, she used avoidance to stay in control. She took time off from work, didn't see her boyfriend for long periods of time and retreated to her apartment as she had to her room as a child. Henry David Thoreau said, "Things do not change; we change."[4] It took a while for Penny to understand her behavior through therapy and start to change.

Penny suffered from a major depressive disorder as well as GAD. I was reluctant to prescribe an antianxiety agent because of her history of poly-substance dependency. I took a history of all the psychiatric medications that she had been given through the years. The one that seemed to work the best was an antidepressant that also had a calming effect. For sleep, she occasionally took a sedating antidepressant often used for insomnia.

I taught Penny behavioral relaxation techniques, including progressive muscle relaxation and deep breathing, which she found helpful. I also encouraged lifestyle changes such as caffeine reduction and good sleep habits. She began to keep a diary, which helped drain off some of her negative energy and angry feelings. I pushed her to broaden her world and reconnect with friends and family. One of the best things that happened was that out of the blue, her old boyfriend called her. He wanted to see her. In therapy, she reported: "When he called, I felt cornered and trapped like I always did with dad. With dad, I used to have to take a (pill) before I saw him. I felt hurt and inadequate. In the past, when Ben called and asked me out, I used to have to drink two margaritas to calm down before I saw him." I had her make a list of how Ben and her dad were the same and how they were different. Apparently, they both had "anger against the world and were judgmental." However, with Ben, she admitted that she felt safe around him and "he wasn't a drunk."

"I want it to work this time [with Ben]. I want to work on the things that make me irritable about him," she said. He often overstayed his welcome and didn't allow her enough privacy. He wasn't always attentive to her and liked to go off and talk to other people when they went on vacation together. He was obsessed with politics and would talk passionately at length on the topic. We discussed ways that she could make the relationship better. She came up with the idea that she could set limits on his behavior, change the subject when he went on a rant about politics and tell him what she needed from him. Most of all, she had to keep focused on the fact that although he had some of her father's behaviors, he was different from her father. I told her to look Ben right in the eye and say to herself, *You are not my father.* If she felt tense prior to seeing Ben, she promised that she would engage in twenty minutes of relaxation exercises rather than having a drink. When her mind drifted back to childhood, perhaps she could refocus and really enjoy being with Ben in the present.

When she started to feel better she stopped coming to therapy, so I called her after nine months. She picked up the phone on the first ring, sounding pleasant and glad to hear from me. "I'm working a lot," Penny said. "Things are the same with the family and the anxiety. Not much has changed for me. I talked to Ben when he was in the hospital but I am not seeing him. He calls me from time to time. Too much time has gone by. I can't go back to seeing him again. I don't have the energy.

"Therapy did help but I got to the point where I felt that I wasn't going any further," she continued. "I was disgusted with myself and I felt that I was dragging you through the mud of my life with me. So I just stopped coming. You tried very hard. I knew that you were trying to tell me things and connect the dots for me. I would get it and then when I left, I couldn't always make it work."

I told her that I thought she was being too hard on herself, that perhaps her expectations were too high and that change takes time. I told her that I thought that she had made some progress. I asked her how her temper was. She answered, "Oh, my temper has been better. I don't let myself get drawn into the chaos at work anymore and I'm not acting out. I guess I did make some progress." I encouraged her, when she felt ready, to return to therapy and continue to takes steps in a positive direction. We wished each other well and hung up.

Susan's Story

"My anxiety is a life-long problem. When I began therapy at age seventeen, I learned that I had been having anxiety attacks going back to when I was five. When I was young, it presented itself as a fear that something horrible would happen to my mother, who is an alcoholic. I could not sleep anywhere but at home. She'd have to come to my classroom and stay until they could pry me off of her.

"As I got older [high school], it took a toll on my physical being. I was diagnosed with irritable bowel syndrome. I barely ate because my stomach was in knots all the time. By my senior year, I was having anxiety attacks. I'd be in class and start thinking that I had to get out of there. I'd feel out of breath, my heart would beat fast and my palms would sweat. These attacks increased three years ago when my mom became ill. I'd feel out of control and my limbs would tingle."

Susan was in her thirties when I first met her. She was a petite woman with green eyes who had been married for thirteen years, with two children and five dogs. Her husband was a salesman who traveled and was away at least one week a month. She described him as "a sarcastic, total hothead," but she felt that they had a good marriage. Susan suffered at times from Temporomandibular Joint Disease (TMJ), irritable bowel syndrome, headaches and a balance disorder. "These physical things are frightening. I'm afraid I'm going to die," she said. Susan had an inconsistent work history and had had multiple part-time jobs.

She described her mother as an alcoholic who was very nervous, overprotective and often depressed. She said that her mother was also controlling, critical, insecure and needy. "She was very etiquette-minded. Everything had to be done properly. She could be a mean and domineering drunk...I was a good kid but was constantly yelled at by my mother…I didn't know what was going to happen day to day." She described her father as a "working alcoholic" attorney, who was prone to anxiety, panic attacks and phobias. He was not affectionate and not home most of the time. She felt that he was in denial about the degree of her mother's drinking and enabled her habit. She had much anger because she felt that her parents protected and supported her irresponsible older brother financially. She resented that they were not as financially generous with her and her family.

Susan had many issues including excessive worry, low self-esteem, shame and guilt. She felt like a victim under pressure. She would often say things such as, "I'm a nervous wreck…I need an attitude adjustment…I take on other people's pain…I'm a worrywart…When things happen to my children, I feel like an awful mother. I feel that I should be doing more." Loyalty was important to her. She often felt weak and helpless even though in high school she was a popular cheerleader: "I was suffering inside. My family taught me to put on a good front." In her childhood home, she had been taught the mantra, "We are Stanfords. We are strong and will get through this." Susan's childhood role in her alcoholic household was to be the caretaker, peacemaker and mediator. This role helped her feel more in control during the chaos. "I used to put up signs all over the house that read 'DON'T DRINK,'" she said. "Holidays were the worst time with high expectations and much turmoil. At least mom wasn't drunk. We gave her fake wine on those occasions."

Susan's Opinion of What Helped Her Anxiety

"I still have a lot of nervous energy, but I've learned to cope with my anxiety better after many years of therapy off and on. I realize now the power my mind has over my reactions to things that make me anxious. A lot of times, I'll say to myself, 'F you, anxiety. I don't have time for you today.' I try not to anticipate catastrophes. I tell myself to go with the simple and not just assume the worst. Therapy has helped me to feel more in control. I'm starting to realize that my parents overprotected my brother because they saw him as weak. They saw me as strong and not needing as much from them. I'm trying not to worry about my kids as much. I try not to listen to the critical policeman in my head. I've learned that nothing bad will happen if I don't please my mother all the time. I don't have to be so demanding of myself.

"I feel better about myself. I even got a part-time job in a hair salon. I'm thinking about looking for full-time work. I still get anxious going to work, because there is a lot of drama there. The chaos reminds me of my childhood and brings back old feelings. When a customer yells at me, I look them straight in the face and tell myself that they are not mom. Overall, I feel more in control. I stopped drinking caffeine. I use breathing techniques a lot. Tai Chi is wonderful. Nature calms me, so I walk outside a lot. It's miraculous to feel that I'm in control of my anxiety now. I honestly thought I'd live trapped by it forever."

My Opinion of What Helped Susan's Anxiety

Like Susan, many people with GAD remember being anxious even in childhood—her school phobia morphed into free-floating anxiety. Educating her in therapy about anxiety and its genetic basis was helpful to her. By using this concept, she was able to separate her anxiety from her negative view of herself and not use it to put herself down. I got her to talk about the shame that she felt not being able to bring friends home, because she never knew how her mother would be acting. As an adult, Susan fretted and worried about her two teenage daughters. Eventually, she began to realize that if her girls were not perfect it did not make her a bad mother. She pushed her husband to take on more responsibility around the house and with the children. She resolved some of her negative feelings about her brother and realized that her parents loved her even if they treated her differently. I helped her look at what they did do for her instead of getting lost in her own expectations. We cannot pick our parents, but we can realize that they are probably doing the best that they can.

Most of all, underlying her anxiety was her ambivalence about her mother and father. She loved them but yet was quite angry at them. Many children will say to a parent when they are angry, "I hate you. I wish you were dead." When she was young, she could not express the negative and tell them how she felt. As a young child, she could not deal with the guilt that expressing her negative feelings would have caused, so in the unconscious, anger equated to killing. She was also fearful that if she expressed negative feelings toward her parents that they would "throw her out in the snow." At that time, she needed them to take care of her basic needs for nurturing and support. She still worried that if she set limits and told her parents that she did not like their behavior that they would cut her off financially. As a child, becoming the caregiver helped her stay in control of her strong emotions and her life at the time. Susan carried this role into adulthood. In other words, she was using an old coping mechanism that may have made sense in childhood but was not necessary as an adult.

Whenever there was chaos, regardless of the setting, she started to feel the same sense of helplessness and inadequacy that she had felt as a child. Susan responded by internalizing her anger into physical complaints such as temporomandibular joint pain, headaches, dizziness and bowel symptoms. She became self-critical and redoubled her efforts to be a better caregiver and peacekeeper. It was difficult to break free of these unconscious patterns. It was hard for her not to return to her self-designated role as the mediator who had to solve all of the family problems. It took a lot of practice for her to start to refocus on the here and now, lighten up and leave these old responses and that little girl behind. I constantly encouraged Susan to remember that her adult world was not the same as her childhood world. She could make other choices.

Medication was also a helpful part of her treatment plan. In the past she had been on various antidepressants and benzodiazepines for anxiety and panic attacks. At the beginning of treatment, I reviewed several options with her and decided to raise her current dose of antidepressant medication, but before long she no longer needed it.

Susan found that Tai Chi dissipated some of her excess energy, anxiety and aggression. The relaxation breathing technique also helped to calm her, as did decreasing her caffeine intake. I encouraged her to continue to ride her bike and play tennis. Her marital relationship worked and she often did these activities with her husband. In spite of her husband's short fuse, he was supportive of her, they had fun together and she knew that he loved her. She still had to get used to her two daughters being normal, imperfect, unpredictable teenagers who were busy with many activities. Susan took a part-time job that gave her great satisfaction and many compliments. She started to ask her parents for what she wanted instead of waiting to see if they would pass her test and meet her expectations. She dwelled less on the past and more on the present. She learned to refocus.

Chapter 4

Step 4:
Lower Your Expectations

Anxious people often ask too much from themselves and others. They tend to take on too much, give too much and expect too much. Lowering your expectations even 10 to 20 percent will decrease your chance for frustration and failure. Your 80 to 90 percent performance will probably still be very much appreciated.

Most people only give 50 to 60 percent at work. It is not possible for other human beings to fulfill your needs 100 percent, particularly those that did not get fulfilled in childhood. If you expect a little less from others, you will be less disappointed and able to obtain a more realistic long-term picture of people.

Expectations are beliefs that are centered on the future that may or may not be realistic. High expectations of themselves and others are often an issue that causes anxious people problems including disappointment, anger and burnout. Make peace with who you are and believe in yourself. Push yourself to do better but accept your limitations. Do a good job at work but don't overdo it; you will limit your options. Your boss will give you more than your fair share of the work since he or she knows that you will get it done. People will come to expect this high level of excellence all the time and will be angry with you on days that you cannot perform as well. Say no occasionally. If you are overloaded with projects at work when your boss assigns you another challenge, tell him or her that he or she needs to give it to another employee and, if the right person cannot be found, to check back with you in a few days and see how your work load is at that time. Life is not always fair. Don't base your expectations on this premise. Author Dennis Wholey tells us, "Expecting the world to treat you fairly because you are a good person is a little like expecting a bull not to attack you because you are a vegetarian."[1]

In reference to relationships, remember that nobody is perfect. You cannot change other people. You can only take responsibility for your own actions and your half of the interaction. We are all human, with good and bad points. Don't just pay attention to see if people are fulfilling your needs the way you want them fulfilled. Also see if they are trying to fulfill them the best they know how, although perhaps different from what you expect. Love is love, regardless of the container it comes in. If you lower your expectations, you may be pleasantly surprised. Psychotherapist Fritz Perls created the "Gestalt prayer:" "I do my thing and you do yours. I am not in this world to live up to your expectations, and you are not in this world to live up to mine. You are you and I am I, and if by chance we find each other, then it is beautiful. If not, it can't be helped."[2] Dan, one of my clients, struggled with many of these challenges.

Dan's Story

"My anxiety can be summed up in two words: expectations and control. When I was younger and very shy, I didn't want to be in situations where I didn't have any control, because I didn't want to do something to embarrass myself. When I was in school, I had anxiety about not being able to control the actions of others so that we all wouldn't get into trouble with the teachers. With my parents' tempers, I was afraid to do anything to set them off and start a fight. I felt helpless and out of control. Now as an adult, I still get anxious and worry over situations where I feel helpless and out of control, like traffic jams, flying and losing my job.

"When I get anxious about a problem, I tend to obsess on it to the point where I can't concentrate on things that I need to do, or I can't sleep because I lie in bed worrying about the problem. I can get so worked up that I feel nauseous and can't eat. I also get irritable and quick tempered. I tend to become quiet and avoid conversation. Sometimes I break out in a cold sweat, get dry mouth or a racing heartbeat, or that hollow feeling in the pit of my stomach that lets me know that I'm about to do something uncomfortable."

Dan was thirty-seven years old but, hunched over in his chair wearing jeans, a T-shirt, sneakers and a baseball cap, he appeared to be about twenty. He made limited eye contact and often just looked toward the side. He seemed like a nice young man who was tense and unhappy. He said that he came for therapy because of "anxiety issues and a lot of things—jealousy and anger." His wife of five years had become friendly with a group of women through the Internet and spent a lot of time chatting with them. He felt rejected and left out. They had a four-year-old son who also kept them busy. My evaluation of Dan showed evidence of GAD, chronic low-grade depression and marital issues. I started him on an antianxiety medication and talked to him about making a commitment to ongoing individual psychotherapy. I also made a mental note to ask him, at a later date, about his expectations of marriage and try to find out why he felt so needy.

After months of therapy, when I asked Dan to write about his anxiety, he was able to share many insights that he had gained about how his early life experiences influenced his behavior and how he became the man he was. He wrote: "I think my anxiety is a combination of both my personality and certain stressful events from my childhood. I'm a very shy person, and so when I was younger, I would get very nervous when I had to meet new people or go to new places. My parents could see that I struggled with my shyness. Their idea of helping me was to force me to do things that made me uncomfortable and 'supporting' me by telling me to 'just deal with it' or 'just grow up.' Their thinking was that I'd learn that it wasn't so bad and that I'd be better off for going through it. However, without guidance and reassurance, instead of becoming comfortable with myself and gaining confidence, I'd just panic because I was afraid that I wouldn't know what to say or do and I'd embarrass myself. I would get asthma attacks, which made me feel even more judged and vulnerable and didn't help my stress. I quickly learned to cope by fading into the background, so that I could remain unnoticed.

"My parents sent me to a private religious school. It was very strict. This was a stressor because I didn't like getting into trouble or being yelled at. In my school, this was a near impossibility, because the teachers used to punish the entire class if one student acted up. I tried to be perfect, never upset the teacher and not be that one kid. A couple of kids enjoyed battling the teachers and constantly caused trouble. This added to my anxiety. I'd get so worked up that I couldn't eat before school.

"Unfortunately, my home life wasn't any less stressful. My father left our home early on. At first, I lived with my mother and grandmother. My grandmother had a bad temper and was a neat freak who spent all of her time cleaning. My mother is very messy. They always seemed to be fighting over cleaning the house. My mother is an 'up and down' bipolar and needed to be hospitalized periodically. She remarried when I was in second grade. My adopted father was an alcoholic and also a neat freak, so they were at each other a lot about cleaning and helping with chores. On top of that, my stepfather did shift work. Because of his constantly adjusting schedule, he could get increasingly irritable when he changed shifts and could snap at meaningless things. One time we were eating dinner when my mother and sister both spilled their drinks. My stepfather got so angry that he pulled off the tablecloth and sent everyone's food flying to the floor. When he was working late shift, everyone had to be quiet. If we woke him up, he'd go off on a mad tear. I was constantly on edge and scared because I felt like I needed to be perfect both at home and at school, so that I wouldn't get in trouble.

"As I take a look back at some of the events that led me down the anxiety path, there is another area that I feel I need to go over. I think that my personality helps to direct my reactions now. During my childhood, a lot of my anxieties were from situations where I didn't do anything wrong. These situations were really the result of other people's tempers or problems.

However, I know now that I took everything so personally. I find it hard to separate my feelings of letting someone down with the reality that the other person's expectations were unreasonable. I know that it's not always my fault. No one should expect a person to act perfect all the time (particularly a child), but I considered it a failure on my part if I didn't achieve perfection. It went from being someone else's unreasonable expectations to having my own unreasonable expectations. I spent so much time worrying about making other people happy that I didn't think about what made me happy."

Dan's Opinion of What Helped His Anxiety

"In therapy, I am learning that I don't always have to be perfect and that I don't always need to be in control. If something happens that embarrasses me, so what? Most people are too busy leading their own lives to notice it, or if they do, they don't know me. In the long run, it won't have any bearing on how people perceive me.

"I've found that with my anxiety, if I get obsessive about a situation that I have no control over, my best remedy is to do something physical like going for a run or shooting some hoops. I used to get frustrated, because I felt that I wasn't getting what I wanted. It helps to lower my expectations and look for the positive. Sometimes, I'll just play a mindless video game that lets me forget about my problems. If I'm stressed about something that I have control over, I'll try and talk out the problem with a friend, so that I can get it out in the open and not let it fester inside. Once I do that, I can take ownership of the issue and set aside some time so that I can come up with a game plan for how to resolve the problem."

My Opinion of What Helped Dan's Anxiety

In therapy, we spoke about Dan's expectations of marriage. Initially, he chose his words carefully and was very hesitant to share his feelings. Gradually, he admitted that he felt angry with and distant from his wife. He resented having to wait his turn when she was texting her friends. "All my life I've been looking for something," he said. "I get down on my wife and other people, because I do not feel I'm getting what I want. I want some positive attention (all I got as a kid was criticism)—a pat on the back, someone to say 'you did well.'" He wanted to do more things with his wife, but hesitated to ask for what he wanted. "I tend to sit around and wait," he said. He didn't have the confidence to take a risk and be proactive. When I suggested that they have a date night each month and take turns deciding what to do, he said, "I don't like making decisions. Maybe she won't like it."

He got particularly distressed when his wife announced that she was going away for three days with her Internet pals. "I got anxious and upset and felt tense inside; I felt left out," Dan said. He agreed that perhaps this reminded him of when his mother left to go to the hospital and brought back many of his negative feelings from childhood. I also commented that perhaps these friendships satisfied his wife's needs and had nothing to do with his relationship with her or how she felt about him. I tried to get across to him that a couple needs to have activities that they enjoy together; however, it is also important for each of them to have activities that they do apart. He started to try things outside of his comfort zone. He joined a golf league at work, he spent quality time with his son, he did a run for the Multiple Sclerosis Society and made arrangements to complete a five-kilometer run to raise money for the local zoo.

Many anxious people like Dan approach something new with trepidation. Their need for perfection causes them to feel overwhelmed, helpless, inadequate and out of control. These feelings, as well as fear of failure, cause avoidance and immobilization. Their need to get it perfect isn't really about perfection—it is about staying in control. If a therapist can figure out where a client feels out of control in his or her life and give him or her a sense of control, it will help. Nervous people like Dan walk through life on a tightrope and often have difficulty moving to the left or to the right. Any loss or threatened loss of control causes them to feel helpless and subsequently anxious. Actually, their life histories seldom show evidence of loss of control. The problem is that they have a need for too much control, not that they have too little control. This is a fine distinction that, if understood, can allow them to feel calmer and more secure.

Dan felt that he was a victim of other people and their problem behaviors. He needed reassurance that he was not helpless. I tried to help him understand what Victor Frankel said in his book, *Man's Search for Meaning*: "You cannot control what other people do to you, but you can control how you respond to what they do."[3] Dan worked on being more proactive and tried to remember to take a problem-solving approach. He gradually learned that one way to feel more in control was to take action. This is one of the best ways to stop the cycle of anxiety and worry. Take charge of your life, examine your assumptions, talk to others about your worries, talk to a mentor who can give you a different point of view. Rather than feeling overwhelmed by health or other worries, get the information that you need to put things in perspective, place yourself on a more positive path and help yourself feel more in control. Dan needed to learn how much control he really had as an adult: he has more resources and knowledge than he had as a child. He can ask for what he wants. He can go out and make things happen. He does not have to wait for mom and dad to do it all.

We also talked about his self-esteem. "I don't feel like I have a lot to offer," he said. Dan had high expectations of what was required of him: "Talking to people sometimes feels like such an effort." He stayed away from group settings: "I don't feel comfortable or adequate enough to do that." I suggested that he talk to one person at a time and not become overwhelmed by the group. He replied, "At age six or seven, when I would try to talk, the adults would interrupt me and not let me finish. Then they would say, 'Why are you so quiet and why do you look so unhappy?'"

Dan's mother added to his already diminished self-esteem. "If I didn't get a summer job or good grades, she always pointed out that my friends had done better," he said. "When my wife started communicating with her new friends, I felt I was left out, because I wasn't good enough to be part of their group. They were better educated, better writers and better communicators than I was. I felt that they left me out because I was inferior."

Certain people in his life "engendered raw anger" in Dan. In therapy, I asked him if he had ever felt this way before, perhaps earlier in life. He immediately said, "When I was four, we went to California with my uncle. He took us to visit Hearst Castle. I didn't want to go. I didn't get a vote. I was furious." I considered this a "screen memory," which focuses on one situation and illustrates a feeling but stands for multiple other instances when the person felt that same thing. Dan then went on to tell me, "It's like when my mom manipulated me to do things that she wanted. She told me lies to get me to do what she wanted. When I was twenty-two, I wanted to move out on my own. She got my grandmother to give me money to buy a car. To her this was a contract to have me stay in the house. Once again, I didn't get a vote…Because of my lack of confidence, I was afraid to push my view. Guilt was her big weapon. She would make me feel guilty in order to get her way. She constantly compared me to other people. Nothing that I ever did was good enough. If something was wrong, I felt that it was my fault." Dan made some of these same assumptions about his wife and because of that, he often felt angry at her.

Dan had a strict internal "rule book" that had been written during his childhood by his "drill sergeant" stepfather. Thinking that there was only one right way to do something hindered his forward movement. He often asked me, "How should I handle it?" I always answered, "How do you want to handle it?" He gradually learned that as an adult, he could take control, review the choices and consequences and make a decision on his own, based on his judgment of the situation and his own needs.

An antianxiety agent twice a day was helpful in reducing his tension and allowed him to use his energy more constructively. I encouraged Dan to make active lifestyle changes including exercise and outreach. This would decrease his feelings of isolation, passivity and inadequacy.

When I first met Dan, he kept his thoughts and feelings inside. When he spoke, afraid of disapproval, he weighed each word before he let it out of his mouth. Therapy gradually taught him that he could share things without fear of criticism, punishment or retribution. One day he reported, "Recently, I heard that there might be reorganization at work. I got worried and anxious about job safety issues. In the past, I would keep it all inside. I would have come home and taken it out on my wife by being anxious and agitated. I would overthink things and have difficulty sleeping. This time, I spoke to my supervisor and coworkers. I heard sympathetic voices and gained perspective. I realized that I wasn't the only one who had these fears. I realized we are all in the same boat. I will try to relax and go with the flow."

Sex was also a problem in Dan's marriage. As with many young couples today who have young children and are both working, they found that fatigue can take its toll and, because of this, sexual intimacy occurs less frequently. As Dan allowed himself to be more verbal, he spoke about "feeling lethargic and in a rut. Our sex life is down. I feel uncomfortable approaching her. I know that she doesn't want to have sex when she comes to bed and puts her heavy fleece-lined sleep socks on." He complained of feeling more anxious, irritable and frustrated. I spoke about his expectations and about his trying to be more affectionate outside of the bedroom. I suggested that he talk to his wife in a positive, tactful way and tell her that he loved her and missed not being intimate with her.

Dan fell back into old patterns of behavior at times. "Sometimes, I still feel like a little kid trapped in an adult body," he said. Therapy doesn't teach you how not to fall backwards. Hopefully, it teaches you how to get out of the hole faster if you do regress. People ask me why they cannot understand all of this on their own. They want to know why they cannot go through Dan's therapeutic process in their own minds and figure it out. The answer is that we wear blinders to our own behavior. Talking it through with someone else who is uncritical and accepting helps you gain perspective. When I looked at Dan much later, I saw a man who was more comfortable with himself and more content with his life. His expectations were more realistic, he was thinking about going back to school to complete his college education and he and his wife were getting along better.

Chapter 5

Step 5:
Express Negative Feelings

Express your negative feelings. Determine if other emotions are underlying your anxiety. You may be suppressing negative emotions. Talk about them with someone you trust; you will not lose control or be punished. Sharing your concerns with someone who can handle them will bring you closer together, not further apart.

Anxiety is said to be "free-floating" or generalized if it occurs in situations where there is no external danger. "Signal anxiety," according to psychoanalytic theory, serves the purpose of alerting the individual to internal danger due to unconscious conflict. Symptoms are believed to be due to unconscious fantasies of punishment for instinctual wishes, originating in childhood, that are socially unacceptable and consciously intolerable. There are four typical dangers that give rise to fear and conflict: loss or separation from a person on whom we depend for love and support, loss of love due to anger or disapproval by such a person, loss or damage to the genitals and conscience- or guilt-driven disapproval of oneself due to one's own moral standards (superego anxiety). The most typical issues involve sexual and aggressive impulses. Psychoanalysts often joke that "it all comes down to anger and sex."

Emotional maturity can be defined as the ability to accept someone's anger and love as well as being able to tell someone that you love them or are angry with them. A number of my clients suffering anxiety, although behaviorally mature and able to handle responsibility (such as paying their bills and taking care of their homes) show some deficit in their level of emotional maturity. For instance, many things make them angry and upset. However, these aggressive impulses are considered taboo. They unconsciously try to prevent them from coming to the surface by producing anxiety and guilt. If signal anxiety fails and the ego cannot initiate unconscious defense mechanisms to prevent these impulses from rising into consciousness, symptoms including recurrent anxiety, physical complaints or other problems may result. Allowing these dangerous feelings to come up to the surface and be expressed in the safe environment of therapy can be most helpful.

Betty's Story

"My anxiety settles in my digestive system. I have cramps and pains in my stomach. I have irritable bowel syndrome and muscle tension. I'm a very ambitious person. I paint pictures and am usually energetic and a perfectionist. Now, I'm tired and overwhelmed. I have a lot of stress. My fifty-seven-year-old daughter is my main source of stress. A few years ago, she said my husband sexually abused her when she was three. This is the biggest hurt. My son is in prison for selling drugs. I'm ashamed. He has some health issues. I'm worried. I don't feel the prison is taking care of him. He is not a bad person. You need a good lawyer to have a chance at getting released, but we have no money. Yet killers get out sooner than my son. The criminal justice system is very unjust. My doctors can't seem to help me. They don't suggest a suitable diet; they just give me pills. My husband doesn't want me to take drugs. The nutritionist said it was all my nerves. My family physician suggested I see you. I've been putting it off. I waited until it got unbearable. I'm worried that there is something terribly wrong with me. That will be my epitaph. 'I worry about everything.'"

Betty started our first session at seventy-eight years old. She had been married for fifty-eight years and had three grown children, a son and two daughters. She was pleasant, polite and she talked and talked. I observed that she was filled with frustration and anger. But she just smiled and continued her list of things that stressed her. I knew my hardest task would be helping her express her negative feelings more directly. If I was going to help her, I would have to allow her to continue to vent her anxiety and negative feelings. I would have to gain her trust and get her to see the connection between her feelings of stress and her physical symptoms.

Betty was a perfectionist and she had high expectations of herself and others. Anything less than 100 percent success was seen as failure. This need for perfection, which was her way of staying in control, often triggered a cycle of anxiety. Over the course of several sessions, Betty continued to enumerate her stressors and made these points: "I don't like to be late. Having to be at a certain place at a certain time is stressful. God forbid if I'm late. If I get a run in my stocking when I'm dressed, it is stressful, so I usually bring an extra pair along. I'm stressed because I have to take sleeping pills in order to sleep. I worry about everything. Whenever it rains, I have anxiety about how bad the water in the basement will be. I have a sister whom I care about, but sometimes she is nice to me and sometimes she isn't. I never retaliate, which causes me stress. I am a peacemaker. When people say things I don't like, I don't respond as I would like to. Because of this, people take advantage of me."

One of her main stressors was her expectations of her eighty-two-year-old husband. "We bicker a lot," she said. "It stresses me that he waits until the last minute to get ready. It irritates me that he always keeps the television on. It's stressful that he always has to play a CD when we are in the car, even though he doesn't always like the CD he is playing. When men retire, they have very little to do unless they choose to do more. My same jobs continue: cooking, washing, ironing, even when I don't feel like it. It's not fair at all. I feel stress, because I believe I am not appreciated for all I do. I like my bed made every day. He likes to go up and lie down and take a nap, but he never fixes it. I had a dream that he allowed people to come in and wreck my bedroom and leave it a mess. I'm very fussy about my house. He feels that I'm being overly fanatical. My husband says that I am negative in my thinking. I know that I am. So I don't like it thrown in my face."

Anxiety occurs in many elderly people, particularly females.[1] The diagnosis can be difficult to make because people over age sixty-five are more prone to physical complaints. They may have sleeping problems which can often signify anxiety. Other diagnoses such as depression, dementia or substance abuse can mask and/or produce anxiety. Primary medical problems may cause anxiety and some medications can cause anxiety-like symptoms. In addition, senior citizens are prone to stressors that can increase their anxiety, such as illness, disability, loss of a spouse, financial distress and social isolation. A direct, empathetic approach such as "That must be scary" or "That must be nerve-wracking" can be helpful to get them to see the connection. Betty's story illustrates some of these issues.

In therapy, she spoke about the fact that she only had one friend who was still living. This one friend recently moved away. "I miss her very much," Betty said. "I used to be able to talk to her about my worries. Whenever I discuss anything that's worrying me with my sister, she tells me, 'Just snap out of it.'"

Betty was a high school graduate who started working at age twelve: "I wanted to play sports but I had to go to work." Many years ago, she worked as an attendant at a hospital in Pennsylvania but stopped, because "It was too much stress." Then she worked for the postal service for four years as a clerk, but stated, "Due to the stress, I couldn't handle it." Since then, she had always worked at least part time. She and her husband still cleaned a friend's house for three hours once a week. She was quite ambivalent and resentful about having to do this. However, she said they did the house cleaning because they needed the extra money.

Betty said, "I have too much to do. People say at your age, what do you have to do? I have so many things to do. It is stressful to have to go to work at my age and struggle to pay the bills. I have to get myself dressed. That takes time. I shop, go to church and visit sick friends. I keep my husband happy (a lifetime job). I visit my grandchildren when I can (they should visit me more).

I have a lot of doctor appointments. I read a lot about health. Every day there is something. My schedule is full. I stay busy. I'm tired of being busy. I am stressed, because of trying to keep up and do what I did twenty years ago, but I can't." When I asked her why her husband didn't do more for her, she said, "He used to be away, driving a truck." When I suggested that she ask her husband to help her with the housework and shopping, she responded, "I don't want him to do that. I'm afraid he'll mess it up." She then thought for a moment and said, "He's retired now. Why should he lie around? Maybe I should start to teach him how to do the wash. If I'm not there (suppose I die in the hospital), I want him to know how."

Once when I tried to point out to her that perhaps she was anxious because of all the angry feelings that she stored up in her gut, she said indignantly, "I don't consider that anger. I don't get angry. I am just a perfectionist. I like things a certain way. If I can't have it that way, I get stressed." Betty was more comfortable saying that she felt stressed than angry and she is not alone in her denial. Many of my clients feel uncomfortable admitting that they are angry. Often I have to teach clients first to say that they are frustrated, upset or annoyed before they are able to actually use the word "anger" to share their negative feelings.

In one session, Betty explained why she had problems sharing her anger: "I wish I could say what I think and not keep it in. Anger makes me uncomfortable. I am a peaceful person. I do anything to avoid confrontation. It upsets me. I don't want people not to like me. My father acted like he hated us. He was never kind. My father was a fanatic—extremely neat. He was very strict and mean. I feared him. He practically never showed affection. My sister, Gayle, said she hated him. He beat her. I felt the same way but I didn't have the nerve to say what was on my mind. If you said something he didn't like, who knows what could happen? He beat my sister so badly.

"My mother told me she resented having me. She was a very nervous person. She beat me if I did something wrong. I would cry for a whole hour before she beat me. My father enjoyed it. He sat back and said 'Get her. If you don't, I will.' My parents were not the type to give you credit for anything."

Betty often complained about her relationship with her sister. She called Gayle on the phone and expected to receive love and nurturing, but all she got was grief and verbal abuse: "My sister has said things that have hurt me—hurt my feelings. I keep it all inside. It's still hard for me to say anything negative." Apparently, her sister had taken on some of the same characteristics as their parents. Betty had what I call "double trouble" in reference to her sister. When she became frustrated with her sister's lack of support and affection, it reminded her on some level of the same frustration that she had experienced with her parents when she was a child and she had a double negative response that was overwhelming to her. It would be helpful if Betty learned what author and spiritual leader Don Miguel Ruiz said, "Don't take anything personally. Nothing others do is because of you. What others say and do is a projection of their own reality, their own dream. When you are immune to the opinions and actions of others, you won't be the victim of needless suffering."[2] Her parents and sister probably acted the way that they did due to their own lack of positive parenting.

In therapy, we spoke about two of her children. I tried to help her gain a better perspective on their behavior. She was very upset that one daughter accused Betty's husband of "indecent acts" and was bringing a case against both of them. "My daughter is a cutter and has multiple personalities," Betty said. "I haven't seen her in ten years. She has spread so much ugliness about us. It's very hurtful. The whole family is being affected. We were so close. All of a sudden, she just turned on us." From time to time, she also mentioned her incarcerated son. She said he had medical problems, gout and hypertension and she was worried about him. She admitted, "I feel helpless. I feel responsible." I tried to reduce her negative feelings about herself by telling her that I also was a parent and could understand her being upset. However, I told her, "Guilt and shame are very powerful emotions. Your daughter has severe emotional problems and is limited. You did not cause that. Your son is responsible for his own illegal actions. People will know that he committed the crime and will not blame his acts on you." Gradually she realized that she was not at fault. Her children's actions and behaviors as adults were out of her control.

Betty's Opinion of What Helped Her Anxiety

"I find that if I stay busy, I don't have a chance to think about the things that stress me. So keeping busy is the key for me. If I didn't have the medicine I would be a mess. With the medication, I am able to handle stress better. I feel calmer. I'm handling things better. My bowels are not as irritable when I take it. It's amazing. I've even gained five pounds. I know now that when I start having cramping that I am anxious and I try to figure out what is bothering me. I suffered stress for years. I probably needed help for a long time. Twenty-one years ago, when my daughter got married, I had such pain, I couldn't eat. I lost weight and thought I was dying of cancer.

"Praying—that helps my anxiety. I really do believe as it says in the Bible, Philippians fourth chapter, verse six: 'Do not be anxious about anything, but in everything by prayer and supplication along with thanksgiving let your petitions be made known to God' (verse seven) 'and the peace of God which surpasses all understanding will guard your hearts and your minds in Christ Jesus.'

"I use a hot water bottle on my stomach when it acts up. When it cramps and hurts, my husband massages my feet to relax me. We have a book on reflexology. When he touches a tender spot, we look it up in the book. It always points to my colon."

What a wonderful exercise in love and affection they had worked out. The tenderness that he showed in massaging her feet and the quality time that he spent with her was just the right warm touch that would help her calm down.

My Opinion of What Helped Betty's Anxiety

In our sessions, Betty brought her own relaxation techniques, her religious beliefs and avoidance behavior, which helped her cope with her anxiety. As many anxious people do, she kept herself constantly busy to avoid thinking about anxiety-producing subjects.

Looking at Betty's description of her parents through psychoanalytically trained eyes gives us clues as to the anger and fear that she must have felt as a child under the care of two unloving and often sadistic parents. Although she does not remember it, she must have felt inadequate, helpless and enraged by their behavior. She not only feared them but at the time was dependent on them for her care, which made the situation even more difficult and increased her feelings of frustration and helplessness. It must have felt like a no-win situation. These feelings, although unconscious, help us to understand how she became the adult who needs to repress her aggressive impulses and compensate by being so nice, so good, so perfect and always following the rules.

As you can see by Betty's view of what helped her anxiety, her insight is limited. However, without being able to define it, she became aware of her dissatisfaction with many elements of her life. Although she was unable to connect all the dots and always see the correlation between her fear of loss of love, her aggressive feelings and guilt as underlying her anxiety, she had begun to see the connection. Gradually she could say, "I usually do not know that I am getting upset. I don't feel the anxiety but then, when I eat, I get the cramping. My colon is like that." Although she realized that her daughter was mentally ill, her world was shattered when she and her husband were accused of sexual abuse. Her son's legal problems generated much guilt in her. She was filled with anger and rage. Except for periods of irritability and bouts of irritable bowel, these feelings went unspoken. I emphasized to her that anger is a normal emotion and it is how we deal with it that defines us. In therapy, she was able to share some of her disappointment, hurt and anger for the first time.

She came regularly for her appointments, seemed to thrive and was grateful for the help. I think that aside from the antianxiety medication, which was very helpful, she appreciated the therapist-client relationship. Her progress reinforced my firm belief that although psychiatric medications can facilitate improvement in mental disorders, it is people working with people on a sustained long-term basis that is equally—or even more—important in maintaining recovery and producing emotional growth.

Betty benefited from my listening to her talk about her stress. She was pleased that I understood her problems and accepted her uncritically.

Therapy allowed her to vent the many issues that upset and frustrated her. These included her husband's behavior, his perceived lack of support, her constant giving but not feeling that she got much in return, her resentment that her economic situation kept her and her husband working part time in their "golden years" and her difficulty communicating with her husband. She constantly told me, "I can't change, that's just my nature." I constantly retorted, "You can try." However, she seemed to appreciate the suggestions that I made and was often able to use them to improve their communication.

On our first visit, Betty showed evidence of depression as well as GAD. Many years ago, her family physician had prescribed an antidepressant for her to be taken as needed and she still used it occasionally. She had never been on any other psychiatric medications. I started her on another antidepressant which has some sedative properties. I spoke to her current family physician and obtained medical clearance to use both the antidepressant and possibly another drug in the future.

The next time that I saw her, Betty was still feeling quite anxious. She admitted that she had not taken the antidepressant I prescribed because she was afraid of the possible side effects and so was taking the old one her doctor prescribed long ago. I told her to discontinue it and started her on a long-acting antianxiety agent twice a day. This proved to be enormously helpful. Betty also had difficulty falling and staying asleep, so she had tried some non-prescription sleep aids on her own. Over the course of time, I tried her on several drugs for her insomnia. One seemed to give her the most benefit. Her mood gradually improved and her anxiety diminished. Her stomach cramps still appeared when she had a "rough week." However, all in all, her gastrointestinal complaints decreased considerably.

She also stopped focusing on her two problem children so much. She stopped taking her sister so seriously. She started being more proactive. One day she said to me, "I told my husband off. I told him I needed him to help me more around the house. I hold it in. I'm too nice and too good. I bottle things up. I'm not happy. I used to do everything for him and now I can't, because I'm tired. I can't be affectionate, because I'm angry at him. He is only doing what I trained him to do. We are together too much." So she started doing more with other people, such as meeting her second daughter for lunch. At our last session, she told me that she had gone for her one-year checkup with her gastroenterologist. He was amazed that she had not been to see him in one year. She told him, "It's me handling all the stress and anxiety." Betty is still staying busy. It is still difficult at times for me to get her to admit that she is angry or frustrated, but we are working on it.

Chapter 6

Step 6:
Take a More Positive View

*Things are not black and white. Be fair in your evaluation of
yourself and the world. Don't magnify your mistakes. Give yourself
and others credit for small successes. Be complimentary.*

Being able to express love or other positive feelings about yourself or others
is another aspect of emotional maturity. David Watson, PhD, a personality psychologist, postulates that anxious individuals have a high degree of
negative affect with a strong fear component, which leads them to focus on
the uncertainties of future events. They experience more negative emotion
and have pessimistic views of the world, causing them to focus on the negative aspects of self and others. They also think a lot about their mistakes and
failures.[1]

Depression often overlaps with GAD. These two syndromes share
many symptoms and both have a genetic vulnerability. Sadness, loss of interest, decreased motivation, changes in appetite, self-esteem issues, feelings of
hopelessness, wishing you were dead and suicidality are more characteristic of depression. Restlessness, tension/irritability, sleep problems, fatigue,
problems with concentration and vague physical complaints often indicate
anxiety. John illustrates these multiple issues.

John's Story

"My anxiety is depressing. I have a lot of anxiety about every-thing. When I am nervous, I'm a basket case. I shake and pace. I bite my nails excessively. I avoid meals or just eat junk food, although I know it is not good for my health. I become very negative and put myself down. I limit my activity. I often do not want to be bothered by anyone at these times and I just want to be alone in the house and sleep if possible. I worry about my health and about money problems. I had my first hospitalization for Addison's disease ten years ago. I never thought I would still be alive by now. I just think about how worthless I am and how little I have to offer. I wish I could kill myself and get out of this world somehow. I can't do it. Even if I tried, I would screw it up and end up with another health problem."

John was one of the most negative clients I had ever met. At forty-three years old, he was aware of his plight but seemed unable to change. He often roamed the bookstore aisles looking for self-help titles that he felt could assist him. One day, he brought me in a book that he had been reading called *Rainy Brain, Sunny Brain: How to Retrain Your Brain to Overcome Pessimism and Achieve a More Positive Outlook.* What he said he learned from the book was that he was an "extreme pessimist." He underlined this passage: "People who are chronically depressed or anxious are especially adept at seeing things in the bleakest terms. With the good things in life leaving little impression, disappointments and failures loom large in the depressed mind."[2] Change was hard for John. He was deeply wedded to his way of looking at the world. Since childhood, he had no sense that he could control his destiny.

"It is never ending," John said. "When something gets straightened out in my life, something new comes along." It was hard to get him to smile. He was always sure that something terrible was going to happen. He was always waiting for the other shoe to drop. "I'm convinced that I will be out on the street in three months," he said. Vague physical complaints included heartburn, nausea, lightheadedness and dizziness. It was a vicious cycle. His physical problems exacerbated his anxiety, which wore him down and made his physical status and depressed mood worse. His distorted perspective was the glue that held all the negative pieces together. However, in spite of this, until he had to go on long-term disability, he had practiced law for many years. He was still an avid reader, liked music and was a huge Philadelphia Phillies fan. He had a number of good friends and was helpful to his relatives in need.

John came regularly for therapy. He had to take two buses and a train to get to my office, always carrying a briefcase or a plastic bag filled with his appointment book, the newspaper, a nonfiction book, a water bottle, a list of his medications and his latest lab test results. Often he could hardly walk, but he insisted on bringing his gear.

His mother died when he was ten. "She was due to come home from the hospital that day," he said. He does not know for sure, but she probably had a heart condition and Addison's disease (adrenal insufficiency). A heart attack killed her. However, as often happens with children, John blamed himself and felt guilty about her death. "Maybe I did something wrong. I was bad. That's why my mother died," he said. His father remarried when John was thirteen to a woman who tried too hard to be a mother to him. He resented her intrusion into his life. This was always a tender topic. One of his constant laments when he first came for psychiatric treatment was his hatred of his stepmother. This was interesting since she was the one who first brought John to me, because of her concern for his welfare. I tried to explain to him that she meant well and was just trying to fulfill the promise that she had made to John's father that she would be a good mother to John. I shared with John what Leo Buscaglia said: "Don't hold on to anger, hurt or pain. They steal your energy and keep you from love."[3]

John remembers his mother being sick and spending a lot of time in bed but not much about her illness itself. He describes her as being a worrywart who was overly concerned about his school work and overprotective. He loved his mother. It was therefore hard for him to accept that some of his anger was toward her, because he felt abandoned when she died. As our discussion about his mother's death continued, he brought me books and articles on the effect the death of a parent has on a child. They included

The Loss that is Forever by Maxine Harris[4] and Erica Goode's *New York Times* article, "Experts Offer Fresh Insights into the Mind of the Grieving Child."[5] These publications served as a bridge to allow him to loosen up some of his memories and discuss some of these feelings. Until then, he had not talked about his mother's death much and never mentioned his anger, sadness and confusion about her passing.

I brought him an article from *The Philadelphia Inquirer*, "Deathly Difficulty: When you know your spouse will die, how do you find the words to tell the kids?" by Stacey Burling. It dealt with the other side of the coin and the problems that parents have telling their children about the death of a spouse. It emphasized the feelings of guilt and inadequacy that parents can struggle with in having "the talk," and ended with the words, "If any of us make mistakes, they came from love. I trust the kids will understand that as well."[6] I hoped that John would start to realize that both he and his father had been in emotional pain and were having a difficult time when his mother passed away.

When I first met John, he had not dated much. He liked a woman from his office, but was reluctant to pursue her. His anxiety was so high, he couldn't make a move. With some encouragement from me, he did start going out to events with her in a group with several other people from work. However, his disability intervened and he never pursued the relationship further. Later, by chance, a woman named Sara picked him up in a coffee shop in town and came on very strongly. She soon suggested that they go away for the weekend to Atlantic City. Sara started asking him for money and then had him co-sign for a car loan. She forfeited and he was stuck with the balance. He was very hurt. For quite a while after his fiasco with Sara, he refused to date. He finally did try online dating, but said that he only seemed to find "wackos."

One day, a woman called him from a personal dating service, representing herself as a matchmaker for single professionals. She offered to fix him up with a girl and said that he would not be charged the service fee. He met and went out with this woman for a while. He bought some new clothes. He got a haircut. They went to the movies and out to dinner. She seemed to have expensive tastes. We talked about his setting limits on what he could afford and he finally did. He seemed to be having a good time. She never invited him into her home. He usually picked her up in his car in front of the house or else they met where they were going. She did invite him to her cousin's wedding. After she took him to the family affair, she stopped taking his calls. Once again he felt hurt and used.

When I mentioned dating to him, he said, "I'm out of the race. Who would want me? I have nothing to offer. I freeze up. I don't work and I'm sick." Every failure reinforced his negative self-view. When something happened physically, such as falling on a bus or in his apartment, he would get furious at himself: "I screwed that up." It was difficult for him to believe that everything was not his fault. I tried to help him stay away from self-pity, because playing the victim is a limiting role. I told him instead of focusing on the negative, try to make a list of three things that are good about yourself or the situation.

Accepting his illness and his disability was one of the hardest things for him to do. He was smart, had completed law school and established his professional identity as an attorney. It was the one area in life in which he felt he had accomplished something. To him, being disabled took it all away. "I went to a law society meeting," he said. "It got me down. All those accomplished people coming from work and there I was a bump on a log. I felt like an idiot." I tried to tell him that even if he was not practicing law, he would always be an attorney. He was embarrassed to meet new people, fearful that they would ask him what he did. It was hard for him to accept that he could just tell them that he was a lawyer who was on disability but who had multiple interests and activities. His constant tune was, "This is not the life I envisioned for myself. I despise my life. It seems utterly meaningless."

John's Addison's disease caused him to have many collateral medical problems that were frustrating to him. For example, he had a propensity for bone fractures and difficulty with his bowels and urine. He was often in physical therapy for various problems. He called it "my continuing medical misadventures." He saw many physicians regularly, including a family doctor, a gastroenterologist, a urologist and an orthopedist. He took over twenty-five medications a day. He had all of his doctors' reports sent to me. They helped give me a perspective about his physical condition. It was hard for him to see the gray areas—that he was receiving good medical care, had long periods of physical stability, would probably live a lot longer and had the potential for a better quality of life than his mother.

John made some gains. Distracting himself and getting involved in the present was beneficial. He started to communicate more with his sister and spent some of the holidays with her and his niece and nephew. He visited his older brother, a schizophrenic, who lives in a halfway house. He stayed in touch with his aunts and cousins. He adopted a cat, which he felt very responsible toward. He worried about her when she got ill: "My cat is the only reason I'm sticking around." I pointed out to him that his good friends (his roommate and neighbor) also need him for support and company. When he was up to it, he did volunteer work one day a week at a local hospital. He was involved in a philanthropic organization and also attended an Addison's disease support group. He went to Phillies games often and occasionally went to concerts with a friend.

John's Opinion of What Helped His Anxiety

"Forcing myself to reach out, to try to get out and socialize, ultimately helps to decrease the anxiety. I also enjoy watching sports or attending a baseball game. These activities help me forget the anxious feelings, at least for the moment.

"I find that reading a good book calms me down. I enjoy listening to music and going to concerts and musicals. I find them relaxing. I enjoy walking, but am often unable to do so for physical reasons. I try to remember to bring my cane when I go on the Philadelphia subway or the Frankford elevated line.

"My religion and belief in God helps at times. Spirituality is a way for me to feel a genuine relief from everyday pressures and this constant health mess that I am in. It helps me be calmer. I visit my parents' graves and say yiskor (memorial) prayers for them in the synagogue."

My Opinion of What Helped John's Anxiety

Since John suffered from both severe depression and anxiety, I ordered an antidepressant and an antianxiety agent. Due to the chronicity and recalcitrance of his emotional symptoms of both anxiety and depression, I added a second antidepressant which can be stimulating and can cause insomnia. He also takes another medication as needed for insomnia. I then added a low dose at night of an antipsychotic agent in hopes that it would calm his nerves. I later substituted an atypical antipsychotic agent at low doses. This has helped stabilize and diminish—but not eliminate—his symptoms.

From the beginning, I felt that one of our goals in therapy was to help him reduce his negativity and guide him toward a more independent and responsible lifestyle. I hoped that this would help to reduce his sense of helplessness, isolation and insecurity. Freudian psychoanalysis focuses on allowing the patient to function at the highest level of psychosexual development. Psychoanalyst Karen Horney speaks of releasing the "real self" with all its potential for healthy growth.[7] Abraham Maslow, PhD, talks about "self-actualization" as a goal to fulfill one's individual potential.[8] Developmental psychologist Eric Erickson talks about the goal of middle age as being generativity versus self-absorption.[9] Utilizing their theories, I tried to get John to move from thinking about himself so much and get more involved with others.

One of the things that we worked on in therapy was to try and get John to accept his disability and move forward. He seemed stuck in anger and depression and was having trouble moving on to acceptance and resolution. He brought in a book that he had been reading called *Life Gets Better* by Wendy Lustbader.[10] He had underlined two paragraphs that he felt related to his situation. One said, "Acceptance of deceased ability is not the same as capitulation. When our customary way of functioning is blocked, we can either rage at what has been taken away or begin to open ourselves to new approaches."[11] In another chapter he underlined, "Occupying the aggrieved position can become an identity in itself. Misery is at least reliable. We can find a bit more bleakness everyday to add to our supply and then spend much of our time calculating our disproportionate share."[12] John could see intellectually that both these statements related to him. However, he was having trouble making the emotional jump from misery to acceptance that is needed to move forward.

As with all clients with low self-esteem, I worked on reducing John's feelings of shame and guilt which, in this case, centered on being disabled. These heavy emotions can be a roadblock to success and cause much emotional pain. They also increase isolation, which is counterproductive for growth. Many of the people whom I see for treatment tend to be too hard on themselves and take 100 percent of the blame. John even blamed himself for having Addison's disease: "I read that stress can bring it out. I was always stressed." I pushed John to think about these issues. What were his assumptions? What was the true reality of the situation? Why did it always have to be his fault? You don't have to feel guilty or punish yourself.

His low self-esteem was one of the main obstacles to him successfully reducing his isolation and expanding his horizons, particularly since he became disabled. He constantly lamented, "What do I have to offer? What would they want with me?" To further improve his feelings of self-worth, I pushed him to get more involved in the world and reach out to and invest more in others. I encouraged him to participate in activities and put energy back into the world. Charity and volunteer work can give much back to us. Doing something that you like will help you meet new people with common interests. Keep in contact with friends, parents and extended family. Otherwise, they will think that you are not interested and want to be alone. I encouraged him to call his sister and see his nephew and niece. I suggested that he continue to call and visit his brother occasionally. I pushed John to go to his Addison's disease group meetings and to get more involved in activities at the temple which he attended.

I worked on trying to get John to take a more positive view of himself and the world in our sessions. When he didn't eat or want to take his medication, his roommate pushed him and was supportive. On his birthday, his friends took him out for dinner. He also had a few other long-term friends who looked out for him. His sister often invited him to her house for dinner with her family. He constantly responded, "I don't know why they care about me." I had to continually prop up John's self-esteem by reminding him that he was a good friend, a good brother, helpful to others, had a strong work ethic and had a lot to share with others due to his knowledge about baseball, Broadway shows, books, etc. I asked him to focus on what he could do and not what his chronic illness stopped him from doing.

We worked on understanding his underlying anger about his mother's death and I tried to give him a better and more positive perspective about his early life. John experienced a true loss when his mother died and felt he was alone in a dangerous world. His brother was schizophrenic, his father usually was not home and his older sister was married and had her family. I tried to help him understand the amount of rage and anger that he must have felt at the time, underneath his mind-set of helplessness. His conflict involved feelings of anger that were sandwiched between the sadness that he felt over the loss of a person whom he relied on for love and the guilt that he felt because he thought that he had caused his mother's death. His main defense mechanism was to repress his feelings of anger toward his mother and displace them onto his stepmother, who made things worse when she insisted that he call her "mom." He also turned his aggressive drive against himself, which is often seen in depression. It took a long time, but when he was ready we were able to discuss these feelings.

When a new health problem arose, his anxiety increased and he regressed emotionally. His mantra became "When I first got sick ten years ago, I came pretty close to dying. But I went to the hospital. Why did I do that? I shouldn't have gone." Lost in self-pity and mired in feelings of hopelessness, he talked about going to a nursing home, although he is not the appropriate age. Once, I heard from his neighbor and friend who expressed his own frustration and sense of helplessness in dealing with John. He wrote, "John constantly eats. His old friend weighed three hundred pounds and passed away. John feels that if he keeps putting on weight that he won't be around any longer. His roommate and I try to help his attitude but it rarely works. We are concerned about him…I'm not sure what to do. At times, he doesn't take his medications. He looks in the obituaries to see if people his age have died. His roommate and I try our best to comfort and reassure him but at times we cannot do a thing and feel helpless." I wrote back, "I know how you feel and I appreciate your concern. You guys do a wonderful job. Perhaps, with John's permission, you can come in with him for his next appointment and we can all talk together."

After I received the e-mail, I told John about it and tried to get him to understand how his behavior affects other people. I spoke to him about how frustrated and helpless and even angry he made people feel when he acted so negatively. At our next session, as soon as he entered the room, he said, "I'm doing a little better. I went to a movie with a friend. Even though I really did not want to go, I called my sister and told her I would be at Thanksgiving dinner. Sometimes we need a kick in the you-know-what. I think I needed it. I dwell on ten years ago and feel how dumb I was to go to the hospital. I realize that I have to let it go and try to go on living the best I can." I was amazed! Perhaps he was starting to learn about the concept of life that motivational speaker Brian Tracy describes: "You cannot control what happens to you, but you can control your attitude toward what happens to you, and in that, you will be mastering change rather than allowing it to master you."[13]

Although John constantly talked about wishing that he was dead, somehow he showed up religiously for all his appointments and tried to remain active, in spite of physical limitations. He got very upset if I could not see him every few weeks. Although I knew that he was a dependent person, I found it hard to talk to him about his need for constant support. I lengthened the time between his appointments in an effort to wean him off treatment. I knew intellectually that his strong religious beliefs and his love for his pet cat kept him from committing suicide. I continued to encourage him to build a life and gave him a more positive perspective on himself with the hope that it would strengthen his self-esteem and increase his emotional independence. I reminded him that his friends, his new family (his roommate and neighbor) and his sister cared about him. I tried to help him gain a sense of meaning and control within his world, which was so frightening and anxiety-provoking to him.

Chapter 7

Step 7:
Don't Worry

Don't worry; you are using up energy that could be used more fruitfully. What will really occur if you are not perfect? Don't assume a negative outcome. When you get that feeling that something bad will happen, don't take it literally. It is just your mind's way of telling you that you are anxious or nervous.

Persistent, excessive and unrealistic worry or anxious expectation is one of the hallmarks of GAD. Worry is uncomfortable and can interfere with concentration and decision making. It is an avoidance response that anxious individuals employ to cope with threats in their world. Although used as a defense mechanism, it really acts to interfere with functioning and further inhibits their lives. Edward M. Hallowell comments in his book, *Worry: Controlling It and Using It Wisely*, that worrying can provide stimulation and excitement for those who are bored. It can also precipitate secondary problems such as depression, social anxiety and demoralization.[1]

GAD individuals worry excessively about minor matters. Their worries focus on a number of events or activities, come in all shapes and sizes and vary with age. The focus of their worry may shift from one thing to another during the lifelong course of the disorder. Children are concerned about family, their competence, the quality of their performance at school or in sports or catastrophic events such as earthquakes and nuclear war. For college students, academic and interpersonal worries predominate. Adults worry about illness, health and injury, family/interpersonal problems, financial/work issues and misfortune for their children. The elderly worry about their health, social relations and finances.

Worriers feel responsible for everything and show a zealous overconcern about themselves and their loved ones. Classic is the nervous mother who anticipates disaster as she waits for her teenager to return home. Typical is the anxious man or woman who is worried that his or her physical symptoms point to cancer. Characteristic is the individual who is sure that he or she will fail despite adequate preparation. Chronic worriers are prisoners of negative thinking. They tend to be pessimistic and have negative thought patterns. They ruminate, brood and stew. They show cognitive distortion. They tend to catastrophize, overgeneralize and overestimate the likelihood of unpleasant events. Their constant fretting clouds their perspective. They are sure that their negative reasoning reflects reality.

People who suffer from anxiety can experience both mental and physical symptoms of anxiety. Any of these symptoms can cause them to start the cycle of fear and will only heighten their anxiety. When they are feeling anxious, their minds do not convey, "You are just feeling nervous." Instead they hear: "Something terrible is going to happen," "You are going to lose control," "You are going to go crazy" or "You are going to die." None of these statements are true. Nothing terrible is about to happen. You will not lose control, go crazy or die. I tell clients, "You will not lose control. Have you ever lost control? Your personality values control so much that you will never allow yourself to go to the other extreme."

I further tell them: "Probably, what you are experiencing is a slight change in your security level which makes you feel as if you are losing control. If anything, your problem is that you require too much control, not that you have too little. You are not going to go crazy. Have you ever gone crazy? Is there any history in your family of psychosis? First episodes of schizophrenia usually occur in the late teens or early twenties. Most episodes of bipolar disorder occur between ages twenty-eight and thirty-two. How old are you? No physically healthy person ever died of anxiety. If anything, an anxiety episode will extinguish itself even without treatment. It may disappear and come back again at another time. Do you know anyone whose high anxiety lasted forever? Has yours lasted forever?"

To interrupt the cycle of fear, I tell my client, "Your mind is talking to you in its foreign language. Translate these thoughts into English. Try to interpret these fearful thoughts to just mean, 'I am feeling nervous.'" If you do not do this, these thoughts or any of the body changes that you feel can cause you to start a cycle of fear and your anxiety will escalate. You may not be able to stop this pattern from beginning. However, hopefully you can stop the cycle somewhere along the way and not allow your anxiety to rise. It is hard for someone with this issue of anxiety not to worry. I joke, "Perhaps you could save up all your worries and just worry at four o'clock." Sometimes being optimistic and telling yourself, "Don't worry. Everything will work out okay," will break the cycle, allow you to feel more in control and allow you to move forward.

Let's start with the premise that worry is very difficult to erase or reduce. However, here are some things that you can do to try and decrease your tendency to worry:

Determine if your worry is productive or unproductive. Productive worry helps you use your energy in a positive manner to problem solve and take action. It can help you get ready to take a test, deliver a speech or give a performance. Unproductive worry tends to produce "what if" imagery. None of us have a crystal ball to show the future. We cannot predict what will happen next. If you spend all of your time worrying about the future, you will miss what is happening right now.

Challenge your worried thinking. Worriers tend to catastrophize. They tend to have negative, black-and-white thinking. Things are not always perfect. Maybe the answer is somewhere in the middle in the gray area. Worriers often concern themselves with "shoulds." To help clients clarify this last concern, I may ask, "According to whom?" Usually the answer is that the "should" is from their own rule book. We bring some of these "shoulds" from childhood. It may take a while to replace them with a more realistic and humanistic approach. Don't let your past define your present. Two different roads can both lead to good places. Try to be flexible and take a problem-solving approach to life.

Look and see what feelings or fears are underlying your anxiety and worries. Some people who worry are trying to avoid feelings of helplessness, abandonment or inadequacy. They may have a very high sense of what is ethical or moral. This may be based on the false premise that they are responsible and have to control everything. It can be carried over from childhood or based on religious beliefs. As I have said often, we are only responsible for our own 50 percent in any relationship. The world is chaotic. Some things are just out of our control.

Take control of time and be proactive. Many worriers tend to have a sense of time urgency that just intensifies their anxiety cycle. If you feel that time urgency controls you, you will be pressured to handle the future right now, which can make you feel overwhelmed. As I've indicated, anxious clients tend to come early for their appointments and worry what I will think if they are late. If they show this behavior it may be one more clue that I am dealing with an anxious client. I always tell them as they fret, "It's okay, you are only human. Human beings are not perfect."

Gloria, one of my clients, is a good example of "the worry machine."

Gloria's Story

"My anxiety is like a butterfly: Life unfolded in a good way, with no real things to worry about, but somehow a worry seed had been sown inside my body, settling down in the middle of my stomach like a growing butterfly. It seemed to produce anxiety about all those things which might go wrong. Telephone calls might turn out to bring bad news. On the other hand, lack of calls from loved ones might also

mean something ominous had occurred. Not being able to reach family members on the phone was likely to mean that something terrible had happened. The more I worried, the bigger the butterfly would grow and it would find more things to fret about. Doctors became people who only delivered bad news. I would go to the doctor—even if it was for a general checkup—expecting to be told that something was terribly wrong. If tests were taken, I would be waiting for the phone call, which I was certain would confirm that indeed something was terribly wrong. When my daughter and son-in-law announced that they were expecting a baby, I was delighted, but the very next thought was 'one more to worry about!'"

Gloria is married and has two children. She was born in Europe but now lives in Philadelphia. Her husband is an executive with a large international company. Although calm during our sessions, she told me that she usually was restless and needed to be busy. She commented, "It's exhausting to be me." Inwardly tense, she constantly waited for the other shoe to drop. Gloria preferred to be in charge and in control. She stayed active with her children's projects, charity work, self-education and traveling with her husband. She came to treatment a year and a half after her mother died. "I feel so tense that I lose concentration for fear that something has gone wrong," Gloria said.

She revealed that she had been anorexic when she was seventeen. She was convinced that her nervousness was all related to eating or drinking. "I'll make a big meal for company or we will go out to eat," she said. "I'm perfectly relaxed and enjoying myself. It can take a few minutes, but soon I feel sick and go into a panicky state. I feel the tension in my stomach and my head. It's always related to something I put down my throat. I'm fearful that it's coming. Once it happens, I can't put the thought away. I think, 'I shouldn't have eaten that forbidden meal. It was the wrong meal.' It eats away at me. Sometimes, it rules my life and I start to avoid engagements."

The women in Gloria's family all suffered from anxiety. "My mother called her anxiety her curse," she said. Gloria was an only child until she was nine. She worried about her mother, who was always depressed and didn't take care of herself consistently, and felt responsible for her happiness. Gloria's mother's energy fluctuated and she was not self-motivated, so Gloria became her cheerleader. She felt that her mother's withdrawal was escapism: "I used to beg her to get up." Gloria feared that if her mother withdrew, she would never get her back. She was embarrassed by her mother and complained that her mother had a lack of pride in herself. "Sometimes, she would get perfect around the holidays and fix up everything that showed to the neighbors. It was chaotic but inconsistent," Gloria said. She reported that she and her mother could always talk to each other, and she often listened to her mother share her worries. In spite of all of this, Gloria reported that she felt loved by both of her parents. However, she admitted that she felt resentful toward her mother and was having trouble "finding peace with a woman I loved, but who didn't meet my expectations."

Gloria's mother seemed childlike and self-absorbed, particularly when she was depressed. At those times, she withdrew from her daughter. Gloria must have felt abandoned. She fought hard to reestablish her connection with her mother. She would comfort her, encourage her, try to brighten her mood and generally nurture her. She acted like the mother she wished she had. She admitted, "I was the mother to my mother." This behavior made her feel more secure. When her mother died, it reopened an old wound and left Gloria feeling fragile and more anxious once again. In her life today, she still fights hard to keep her connection with her husband and her two children. She needs them to feel secure and in control. She worries constantly that she will lose them. Although she did not always believe it, Gloria is a capable woman.

She described her father as very strict, but liked the fact that he took pride in himself and kept himself busy. She said that he was supportive, loving, caring and always there for her. She felt that both her husband and her father fit in her life well.

Gloria's high expectations and perfectionism often made her life difficult. If her children were not motivated to do something that she thought was important or were not doing well in school, she would try to be helpful and exert subtle pressure on them and the school. If things were not going in the direction that she wanted, she would take over and find a way to make it happen. She admitted, "If I didn't do anything it gnawed at me; I would think about it and couldn't put it down. I could feel my stomach tightening up. I'm scared. I feel guilty. I spend so much time doing it and thinking about how I can deal with it."

Gloria's Opinion of What Helped Her Anxiety

"I can see clearly how unproductive all this worrying is. It takes up valuable time and has a paralyzing effect, which lasts until I know the outcome of the situation. Distance from the concern and being with other people help divert my worries. Once I know the outcome, I do seem to be able to deal with it in a competent way.

"The medication I take is helpful for handling everyday things. I keep the dose light. However, when I get really anxious, the feeling is stronger than the medication. For instance, my daughter is pregnant and she works from home. I call her on the phone. If she doesn't answer, I start to worry and think. 'She is on the fourth floor, she is all alone, what happens if she trips?' I am very excited about her giving birth but I will be very glad when we are on the other side. I don't deal with some things well, but nobody knows it. I may mention it to my husband, but I have practiced through the years not to let it show. People who know me would never suspect that anxiety was an issue in my life. I also cope by having a rational talk with myself and asking myself, what is the real chance of something going wrong? I try to cope by putting the situation in perspective. If I was in the same situation with a neighbor or friend, I wouldn't get so anxious. Lastly, I divert my thoughts to something that requires serious thought and concentration.

"I grew up with a mother who suffered the same way and shared her concerns with me. My mother was extremely anxious and I absorbed it. I have not done this with my children and am able to appear calm on the outside, which I consider a success. However, I would like to be kinder to myself inside—calm those butterflies and give us all a rest. I still feel the butterflies stirring as I am visiting a place I prefer to avoid."

My Opinion of What Helped Gloria's Anxiety

Gloria did well at first on a sedating antidepressant, which improved her mood and helped reduce her anxiety. I later switched her to an antianxiety agent. Initially, she took it regularly. However, after a while she switched herself to an as-needed regimen. It was hard for her to accept help. She only came for a session when she was in great emotional distress. Most times, Gloria saw herself as a competent, strong woman who constantly had to fight her "demons." She was indeed a competent woman with many positive traits, but deep inside was also an insecure little girl who felt that she had to constantly hold onto someone else as a life raft. In therapy, I worked hard at getting her to give up her belief that food ruled her life and caused all her problems and that they were all physical in nature. Gradually, she started to understand that anxiety was the real culprit: "My stomach is the center of my emotions." It was hard for her to give up her feeling of control, share her demons and reformulate her beliefs, but eventually she allowed herself to admit that she felt frustrated and angry at times.

Underlying some of Gloria's worry was her fear that she was an inadequate wife, mother and person. She felt responsible for everything that happened. Her overconcern about these worries caused her to run faster and faster to prevent anticipated disaster. As a child, when her mother was ill, she must have felt vulnerable, helpless and responsible. She feared feeling this way again, which fueled her overconcern about health issues. She feared going to see a physician and remained breathless until she obtained the results of each medical exam.

It was hard for her to accept others helping her. She is an example of the conflict between independence and dependence that often plagues anxious people. Anxiety-prone individuals treasure their independence and resist acknowledging their dependency needs. They are often reluctant to accept help and instead take the teacher or caregiver role. We all need emotional support at times. It is not a sign of weakness, but rather a clue that we are human. Anxious people are usually not aware of how much they need other people. They may have had difficulty with separation early in life and may show particular distress at divorces, threatened losses or the deaths of significant others.

Although she was very good at taking care of others, Gloria slowly started to understand her own need for support and her fear of loss stemming from her childhood. I had to emphasize the fact that even though all strong people need support at times, she really was a strong, accomplished woman who could do well by herself and didn't always need a psychological safety net or have to know where her family members were at any given second. She learned that there was a difference between feeling helpless (as she had as a child) and *being* helpless (as an adult). As a grown-up, she had many resources and knowledge that she did not have as a child. She realized that she did not have to constantly overcompensate. She also needed to realize that she was human, could not always be perfect and would sometimes feel anxious in spite of her drive to control it and make it disappear. She became more comfortable with her anxiety. She realized that she did not suffer from the same illnesses that affected her mother.

I saw Gloria again six months later. Her butterflies were flapping their wings rapidly. She was delighted to tell me that her daughter had a baby boy but had been ten days overdue. She had been very active entertaining and visiting friends and family members. However, she did admit, "Life has been a little stressful with my neurotic kind of personality. I get so nervous. I'm always waiting for the other shoe to drop. I am so focused on the negative. I have a useful brain if I just took the time not to worry."

Her health fears had kicked in again and, like her mother, she was worried about "going to the mailbox to get doctor results to see if [I am] going to live or die." She told me that she had been having vague joint symptoms. She was seeing a rheumatologist. Her husband had also been ill with a serious urinary tract infection. She had gotten a mammogram and was nervous for three weeks until she heard the results. She admitted she had been having butterflies in her stomach and felt scared. She still had not gone for the bloodwork that I had ordered six months previously. At the end of our session she promised to send me her bloodwork. On the way out, with a big smile, she proudly showed me a picture of her handsome new grandson.

Chapter 8

Step 8:
Take Action

Be proactive. This is one of the best ways to stop the cycle of anxiety and worry. Don't let these negative and scared feelings stop you. Take charge of your life. Get the information that you need to find out what your feelings are really all about. Rather than feeling overwhelmed, prioritize and get the job done, one task at a time. Avoid avoidance. Take a problem-solving approach to life.

Many people who suffer from anxiety take a passive approach to dealing with it, because they often do not understand it. They act like victims, feel helpless, fight hard to stay in control, avoid and worry. I strongly believe that, to help themselves, they must learn to take active, problem-solving approaches to their lives and prevent the cycle of fear from escalating their anxiety. They have to learn new coping mechanisms, put things in perspective and find small areas over which they do have control, then build on these successes. This is even more difficult when they have an overlapping condition such as panic disorder. Catherine is an example of this conundrum.

Catherine's Story

"My anxiety is split into two different boxes. The lower level I call stress. The higher level is a full-blown panic attack. The difference

is that stress or anxiety usually has a trigger in my real life—something that bothers me, angers me or scares me. I feel nervous and have various physical symptoms. I shake and my stomach is in a knot. I experience shortness of breath and rapid heartbeats. I feel as if I am going to die or that something terrible is going to happen. Sometimes, life in general is just too stressful for me. I wake up in the morning stressed and I cannot sleep at night because of stress. As a consequence, I sometimes spend most of my day alone in my room, reading, playing on the computer or doing number puzzles, de-stressing and avoiding more stress.

My panic attacks come out of the blue. They last several minutes and are very frightening and physically draining. I feel like I might literally die, because my heart beats so fast and hurts so much. I have trouble breathing and shake uncontrollably. I can't always think rationally and only want to get away from the situation. Some of my panic attacks are so severe that it makes me nervous just thinking about them."

Catherine is not unusual. Many people who suffer from GAD also have another condition such as panic disorder, social phobia or obsessive-compulsive disorder. This is called co-morbidity or symptom overlap. Anxious people are more susceptible to other emotional and physical disorders as well as other anxiety disorders and depression. They may show overlap with various medical conditions such as irritable bowel syndrome, asthma/COPD, thyroid disease and pheochromocytoma.

Anxiety attacks and panic attacks are two different animals. An anxiety attack is usually related to something happening in your life at the present time. You may have vague physical symptoms, often involving various systems of the body. These can include muscle tension, overstimulation of the nervous system and signs of over-alertness. Mental symptoms may include a feeling that something terrible is going to occur, you are going to lose control, you are going to go crazy or you are going to die. The physical and emotional symptoms, as well as the length, may vary from attack to attack.

An anxiety attack may last from a few minutes to several hours. A panic attack, on the other hand, comes out of the blue and always has the same set of physical and emotional symptoms. The length is always the same. If your first panic attack lasts two minutes, all of your panic attacks will last two minutes. It is important to understand this. With this knowledge, you can wait it out, because you know it will stop in two minutes. Be aware that the same person can have both panic and anxiety attacks.

Those suffering from GAD do not report the sudden spikes of anxiety level seen in panic disorder. Those with panic disorders will see their attacks as unique events involving a sudden, massive increase in anxiety which quickly subsides. The person with GAD will talk of a more gradual onset and a less severe intensity. However, their anxiety attacks can last a longer and more varied period of time.

People with panic disorders suffer from anticipatory anxiety. These individuals develop varying degrees of nervousness and apprehension between attacks and become fearful that they will have another panic attack. This does not mean that they will have one. They may indeed only be having an anxiety attack or nothing at all.

In my book, *Panic Disorder: The Great Pretender*, I explain that panic disorder clients can also develop avoidance behavior such as phobias, particularly agoraphobia[1] (the abnormal fear of being helpless in an embarrassing or inescapable situation that is characterized especially by the avoidance of open or public places).[2] To prevent the phobias that can be complications of panic disorder, I clearly and forcefully tell clients that the situation or place (car, supermarket, bridge and so forth) that they associate with the panic attack is not the cause of their emotional response. It is only a place where an unpleasant experience occurred and avoiding such places only exacerbates their problems.

When I met Catherine at her first session, I knew quickly that I would have difficulty engaging her in therapy. She appeared calm and in control, but underneath there burned a volcano of tension. She started our first session by saying, "I'm a very nervous person anyway, but now I am upset and nervous. I can't turn my mind off." She was a private person who valued being in control. It was difficult for her to share that she was worried about her eldest daughter (who had a serious mental illness, was pregnant, unmarried and in danger of losing her job). My initial evaluation showed that Catherine had become progressively more depressed over the last few months. She also felt guilty about her daughter: "Guilt is my middle name. I feel guilty about so many things." Her energy was diminished and her interest and motivation to do things were low. She had difficulty falling and staying asleep, her libido was low, she was having pains in her stomach, had lost her appetite and was experiencing shortness of breath, headaches and palpitations. She was worried and avoidant. She had temporomandibular joint syndrome, muscle tension and bruxism (grinding the teeth at night).

At a later session, she gave me an example of a recent anxiety attack: "My family was here for Christmas. Because there were so many people in the house, I was able to go upstairs to my bedroom from time to time and decompress without anyone missing me. They all know that I am nervous and need time-outs. I was stressed because of the number of people in the house but I was surviving. Since things were going so well, I invited my neighbor, a single woman who had nowhere to go for the holidays, for dinner. Everything was fine until the weatherman predicted a blizzard. My daughters and their families were out of there in less than two hours. The thought of entertaining someone for several hours alone, except for my husband, led to a major anxiety attack. All I had to do was make the string beans. Everything else was done. Making string beans is an easy job. However, I could not do it. I could not make my hands work. They started shaking. I could not control them. My legs also started to shake. My stomach had a knot in it. I experienced the usual shortness of breath and rapid heartbeats. I had to get away. I managed to call my daughter [who] lived the nearest and she returned to help. She finished cooking dinner and covered for me while I went to my room, got into bed and put the covers over my head. This was one of my worst anxiety attacks to date and the reason I have come for treatment."

In future sessions, she would announce, "Well, that's enough," and get up to leave even if there were fifteen or twenty minutes left in her session. She was very up front about the roadblocks that stood in the way of her sharing her feelings and problems: "I'm fine. I beat myself up. I'm not going to tell you my problems. I don't want people to tell me what to do. I don't like to show weakness. People will use it against you." She often apologized for simple things that did not need it. She was prone to stopping therapy for a while and then writing me an e-mail asking for an appointment. Several months into therapy, she wrote, "I have been more nervous than usual lately. Perhaps I should see you about changing or increasing my medicine. I have nothing to be unhappy about. However, sometimes I am a little down. What worries me, however, is my anxiety or nervousness. My husband gets on my nerves. The girls get on my nerves. The grandkids get on my nerves. Not all the time but enough. Obviously, it is not them but me. (I'm giving them the benefit of the doubt.) I try not to show it. I hope that I am doing a good job. In the meantime, I would like an appointment. August 4th, 5th, 7th, 8th, 11th, 12th or 15th between 9:30 A.M. and 11:30 A.M. works for me. Please e-mail me an appointment time that is convenient for you."

People prone to anxiety employ avoidance as one solution to cope with the possibility of emotional discomfort. They hesitate to participate in situations that make them feel nervous. They are reluctant to venture forth due to free-floating anxiety, nervousness, fears and general trepidation. Anxiety is the great inhibitor. It prevents people from living their lives to the fullest. One of my clients once said, "Don't do it again. If it doesn't work the first time, don't ever try it again if you don't want the same feeling to come back." Panic-prone people in particular are vulnerable to passive avoidance behavior. They often channel their feelings into activity or concentrating on others. In conversation, even in therapy, they will focus on anything but what is really bothering them. Catherine described this negative coping skill well when she said:

"Avoidance, avoidance, avoidance is the one way that I deal with stress. Over the years, I have identified things that make me nervous. For example, I avoid crowds, shopping malls, parties, driving on highways, driving at night and driving to unfamiliar places. If I believe that a situation will be too stressful for me to handle, I will do everything in my power to avoid it. If I find myself in a stressful situation, I make an excuse and leave. Last year, my husband and I left a New Year's Eve party that we could not get out of attending after two hours. We told the host that we had promised to baby-sit for our grandchildren. This, of course, was a lie. At every family reunion or similar function, I take my exercise clothes and books. I use them as excuses to leave the house and go walking alone or go to my room and be by myself."

If you are suffering from GAD, avoidance is a poor coping mechanism that can interfere with the quality of your life. If you are suffering from panic attacks, avoiding a certain setting will not stop them from happening. They can happen in any location.

Catherine also complained about her husband: "He is a social man. It makes me nervous. He wants me to go with him. I tell him, it's your thing. You do it...He won't travel, which angers me. I want to see more of the world...He never helps me. I have to pick the grandkids up from school so that my daughter can work."

I suggested that she ask her husband for help. I told her, "Men sometimes do not volunteer. However, if you ask them to do something and they do it then you do not have a problem." Self-esteem was another discussion point in therapy. In time, she admitted that she felt insecure and said, "I'm a fake." This made her feel overwhelmed, anxious and out of control. She compensated by trying to be in complete control.

Often she adjusted or stopped her medication on her own. I explained to her that I was not her father, her priest or a judge. I could only give her my professional recommendations and the reasons for my advice. All I asked was that she consider my suggestions and see if they were right for her. She was a grown woman and had to make up her own mind about what she wanted to do. Her initial response was often, "No, I do not want to do it." Sometimes, she would think it over and change her mind. After one difficult session in which I tried to explain why I felt that she should continue her medication, she wrote me the following e-mail: "After reviewing my options, I have decided that it was not in my best interest to discontinue both the antidepressant and the antianxiety medication at the same time. I would like to keep taking the antidepressant for the recommended two-year period and reassess the situation in six months. Please call in a prescription for me at the drug store. I will take the appointment at 2 P.M. on December 19th so that you can assess my progress."

The focus of many of our sessions was to encourage Catherine to be more proactive. She was passive in asking for what she wanted. She was also passive in her avoidance. She internalized her emotions. In spite of her initial reluctance, I knew that becoming more active in her behavior and responses would help her feel more in control and reduce her anxiety. We also worked on her ability to say "no" when people placed demands on her that caused her to overextend herself, subsequently increasing her anxiety. "I have to stop worrying about what people think about me. I feel guilty if I say no," Catherine admitted.

After several months of therapy, she related this example of trying to be proactive. In a way, it had a happy outcome: "My neighbors would not stop talking about the new supermarket that opened up fifteen minutes from my house. The brand of coffee that I love was out of stock in all three of the stores where I usually shop. I didn't like leaving my comfort zone but I wanted the coffee. The trip to the market was uneventful. I did not feel stressed. I walked into the foyer of the store and the automatic doors leading to the main part of the store opened. I looked into the cavernous interior of the store and saw what looked like hundreds of people. They looked more like ants crawling out of and over an anthill rather than people shopping. The noise was a loud, overpowering cacophony. The aisles, instead of being straight, were at odd angles like blocks thrown to the ground by a giant child. It was utter chaos. There were too many choices. There were too many people. My heart started beating fast, my stomach cramped up and I could not get my breath. I decreased sensory input by backing into the far corner of the foyer and closing my eyes. I did not think that I could make it back to the car. I knelt down and started my breathing/relaxation exercise and pep talk while pretending to look at whatever it was that they had on sale in the corner. Surprisingly, the attack passed quickly and I was able to go into the store and get the coffee."

Catherine's Opinion of What Helped Her Anxiety

"When I find my stress level rising, despite my best efforts to keep it under control, I isolate myself and simultaneously do deep breathing/relaxation exercises, while trying to rationalize with myself. I tell myself, *It is okay. Everything is going to be okay. Calm down. You can do this. You are worrying about nothing.* Depending on the situation, I will add affirmations. *Why are you so nervous? You are so lucky. You have so much to be thankful for. You have a great husband and wonderful children.* I also block out or decrease sensory input. If removing myself from the stressful situation is not possible, I go straight to deep breathing/relaxation exercises and pep talks. I try not to use avoidance or isolate myself. I know that these methods are really counterproductive. I am working hard to remove them from my list of coping methods when I'm stressed.

"If I get nervous, I get into this cleaning mode...The pills really help... I get a massage every week. I'm going to try yoga. I do best if I have a few hours of downtime. I go to my room and sit in my nice recliner with my feet up. I use my electronics [computer, tablet]. I watch television. I [solve puzzles]. I read for my book club. I don't have to think about anything."

My Opinion of What Helped Catherine's Anxiety

Education was the first item on my treatment plan for Catherine. Sometimes our anxieties are exacerbated by too little or incorrect information. She had to be taught the difference between anxiety and a panic attack. As I've said, a panic attack lasts a specific amount of time. If you know this, you can wait it out and not try to escape. Isolation and avoidance were two of Catherine's main coping skills, but they didn't help. Our mantra became "avoid avoidance." Take a risk and keep moving forward. I also encouraged her to vent her feelings of irritation in therapy. Often a client will not let go of an irrational fear. Their anxiety is covering up some deeper fear that they are unwilling to put into words or are afraid of facing. If Catherine allowed herself to engage in more social interaction, she might find that she could feel vulnerable and imperfect like the rest of us.

Her sessions focused mainly on her worries, her physical complaints and her family problems. She did appreciate being able to vent in a noncritical environment. After one such session, she sent me this e-mail: "I feel so much better now that I have gotten things off my chest. However, I need to vent some more. My husband and I had a long talk and he will help me with the grandchildren. If you have an appointment slot, please let me know."

I worked on giving Catherine a different perspective about a number of things. She felt guilty about her daughter's emotional illness, but I got her to understand that it probably was genetic and she had not caused it. She spoke about "feeling bad" when she didn't do what she felt was expected of her. She said "I'm sorry" much too often. She allowed other people to get her to do more than she felt comfortable by "guilting her." Gradually, she was able to reduce her painful feelings of guilt.

It would take a long time for her to gain insight into the unconscious causes of her tension. Her anxiety made her bolt whenever we got near a touchy subject. She may never understand that much of her anxiety was due to issues in her childhood. She had been raised by two people who only finished the third grade, held menial jobs and produced two schizophrenic sisters for Catherine. Her mother was nervous and aggressive while her father was a nice but passive man who had a good work ethic. She admitted that her mother had high expectations and a "Jekyll and Hyde" personality. In spite of my gentle probing, she avoided sharing much of her background with me. She admitted that she had a problem opening up to others. She acknowledged that she was insecure and felt like a fake.

In spite of her ambivalent commitment to treatment and her lack of psychological mindedness, Catherine made progress. She was placed on both an antidepressant and an antianxiety agent. Initially, she had been on an SSRI for its antidepressant properties, its ability to stop panic attacks and its sedative effect. However, she complained of feeling fuzzy-headed and having a decreased libido. She was changed to another drug which, although it will not help panic attacks, does not have any sexual side effects. She tolerated it well and her sexual interest returned. Her antianxiety medication alone was able to stop her panic attacks and reduce her GAD. She also used a medication for insomnia.

Medication improved her mood, calmed her anxiety a bit and stopped her panic attacks. She slept better. She used her newfound energy to try to be less avoidant and more proactive. She was still hard on herself and others: "I never forgive or forget." She still tended to worry a lot. However, over time she added activities to her life. A literature major in college, she joined two book clubs. She started delivering food one day per week for Meals on Wheels. She jogged daily with a neighbor. She was planning a cruise to the Panama Canal with a friend. At our last session she said, "I'm doing something every day. It's great." I counseled her to keep moving forward, to take control of her life and not to let her anxiety limit her potential.

Catherine was due to see me again in three months. One day, I received an e-mail from her asking me to cancel her next appointment. I e-mailed her back thanking her for letting me know her decision but telling her that I would have preferred that she came off of the medication with psychiatric supervision. I wished her good luck and told her to stay well. I was not surprised at this outcome. Catherine had always been the type of client who resisted taking medication and preferred to solve her mental health and other problems herself. She will always have a need to be in control of her situation.

Chapter 9

Step 9:
Take Things as They Are

Accept that you tend to be anxious. You probably are predetermined to develop anxiety and worry due to a genetic vulnerability. Don't see it as the end of the world. You won't die or go crazy. Accept yourself and others as imperfect and human. Don't try to change everything and everybody.

People who are anxiety-prone resent their apprehensive feelings. They often are self-critical and feel guilty about being anxious. Some psychiatrists theorize that they have the "worry gene" and have inherited this tendency. Clinical psychologists Charles Elliott, PhD, and Laura Smith, PhD, in their book, *Overcoming Anxiety for Dummies*, take a more positive attitude. They say, "Anxiety happens. It will return. Welcome it with open arms. It means that you're still alive. Appreciate the positive aspects. Anxiety tells you to pay attention to what's going on around you. Go with the flow."[1] This is good advice.

Those who constantly feel anxious also overvalue their independence and feel great discomfort in acknowledging their dependency needs or the benefits of a support system. Often, they are reluctant to accept help, preferring instead to be teachers or caregivers. Usually, they are not aware of how much they need other people. They may have had difficulty with separation early in life and may show particular distress at time of separation, such as during a divorce or the death of a significant other.

In spite of this need to maintain the status quo, they are prone to try to change others, particularly significant people in their lives. Marriages or significant relationships become a push and pull to try and remake the partner into the image that they want. It is hard for them to just accept people as they are. This often causes relationship strife. Author Wayne Dyer wisely said, "Love is the ability and willingness to allow those that you care for to be what they choose for themselves without any insistence that they satisfy you."[2] Andrea's story illustrates these issues.

Andrea's Story

"My anxiety is people that I love. They are the ones that mean something to me. Other people outside my inner circle I can put into perspective. I believe that many times my anxiety is stress related to my home life and my job. My home life can be very stressful because I am a talker and my husband is very quiet. It drives me nuts. I'm always trying to get him to communicate and talk to me. I worry that something will happen to him when he goes away on business. I worry about my children. My daughter is twenty and was just diagnosed as clinically depressed. She also has anxiety and panic attacks. My eldest son, age thirteen, is quiet like his father. I often feel disconnected from him because I don't know what he is thinking. My third child is two and a half and is very free spirited, so he is a handful. I'm very protective of all my children.

My mother and mother-in-law both live with my family. My mother-in-law has the beginning stages of dementia. My mother is very supportive, but she also sometimes follows me from room to room, which is okay most of the time. However, sometimes I just like to have my own space. Finally, my father is in prison and has been there for most of my life. I visit him every other week. I don't tell people about him and his situation, because it is very embarrassing to me. My life is full and it is very hard for me to balance everything. At the same

*time, I like order and have the tendency to be a perfectionist, which
makes it all much harder.*

*My job is very fulfilling and at the same time very demanding.
I'm dealing with diverse personalities. I feel like I'm being pulled in
so many different directions. I'm a pleaser, which adds to my stress.
They ask me to do a lot, because they know that I'll do it. If there is a
problem at home or at work, I try to fix it.*

*My anxiety presents with racing heartbeats and sweating. I
get symptoms such as diarrhea and constipation. I feel nauseated. I
become irritated and have trouble sleeping. In the past, I often cried
in the moments that I spent by myself on my way to pick up my
youngest son from day care.*

*When I'm under stress, I have lashed out at the ones closest to
me. For the most part, I lash out at my husband. I don't like being
anxious. It's crippling at times. I don't know what to do with it. I
feel restless. I don't like the way it makes me feel and act. I don't like
myself at those times. I feel like I'm being mean. I like to be happy."*

In our first interview, Andrea explained that she had trouble with trust
and communicating with her husband. They had been together eighteen years
and married for three years. She had a degree in Business Administration and
had worked for a large corporation for more than a decade. Recently she had
been given a promotion, which added to her stress. The stress of this additional responsibility brought to the surface two old traumas. It took a long
time for Andrea to trust me enough to share them with me.

Initially during my evaluation, she described her father as very intelligent, affectionate, loving and expressive. Almost as an afterthought, she
added, "My dad was incarcerated most of my life. He went to jail when I was
seven." In therapy, she gradually spoke more about her father, "The thought
of him can make me cry. He's my dirty secret. He used and sold drugs." She
finally shared how she had been teased when she was young, because she
had a "jailbird" dad: "I always felt that I had to prove something." Andrea
eventually admitted that she was angry at her father and resented him for

not being there for her when she was young. She felt that he had been very selfish. I asked her to write a letter to her father telling him all this, then not mail it and instead bring it to therapy sessions. Writing your feelings down in the form of a letter to yourself or others or keeping a diary is often helpful. It is particularly beneficial in allowing you to express and dissipate negative feelings. Andrea wrote the letter and gave me feedback that it helped her feel a little better.

Several months into therapy, in a torrent of tears, Andrea told me her biggest secret: "I got pregnant at age sixteen. I was immature, rebellious, young and dumb. I had a chip on my shoulder about my father. The guy [who got me pregnant] was attractive but also abusive. After I got pregnant, he hit me. He threatened to take the baby. He threatened to kill me and the baby. I was afraid of him. In the back of my mind, I'm still afraid that he will hurt me. My mother was supportive but made me tell everyone. She is very stable and loyal but not affectionate and can be spiteful. She was very strict but I always felt loved. Now, I feel guilty." I asked Andrea to write a letter to the man with whom she'd been involved and bring it into therapy so that we could discuss it.

At our next session, she said that she was avoiding doing the assignment. We talked it through. The main roadblocks to her writing the letter were her feelings of anger. "I should be able to leave it behind," she said. She didn't like being angry. She was turning these feelings against herself and feeling depressed, guilty and upset: "I don't like to be angry. I like to be happy."

I told her, "Let's try for contentment. Nobody is happy all the time."

With this, she let out the following free-association diatribe: "How could [my boyfriend] do it and have a child? He professed he cared so much but he didn't come to visit our daughter. He would call and say that he was coming and then wouldn't come. It hurt me to see her hurt. If you have problems with me, don't take it out on her. With him it was raw. We would say stuff we didn't mean and then you can't take it back. To acknowledge that he hurt me could have made it worse. I wouldn't be as perfect. I wouldn't be the best person that I can be. I should never hate. I failed everyone."

In return, I said, "You seem to be beating yourself up and punishing yourself. How much penance do you have to pay?"

At our next session Andrea said, "I spilled a lot of beans last time. I never addressed it before." She went on to talk about how and what she would tell her daughter. I think that she was beginning to understand what motivational speaker Tony Robbins meant when he said, "It is not the events of our lives that shape us, but our beliefs as to what those events mean."[3]

Andrea's Opinion of What Helped Her Anxiety

"I have found new ways to deal with my anxiety. I work out daily, which helps to reduce my tension level. I watch my diet and have lost twenty-four pounds in the last four months. I have more energy. Things are just easier with my husband now. I'm talking less. When I shut up, he actually talks. My inside is starting to match my outside. I am trying to live more in the here and now. I used to feel agitated all the time, although people said that I looked cool on the outside. I feel more confident and more relaxed now. We are starting to enjoy our time together again. I tell the family when I am becoming anxious so that they can give me time to myself. At work, I am trying to be different. I used to try and come off strong with my co-workers. I would never say no. I felt that I had to be good all the time. All it did was make me feel burnt out.

"I have recently started to reconnect with a couple of old friends so that I can plan time away from the family. I'm making myself little bridges. I feel more connected. I shared stuff with a woman at work. I couldn't believe it. She had experienced some of the same problems. I felt better talking to her. It took a load off of my shoulders. I used to be a little island by myself. I realize now that with the right person, it is good to share. I was always very closed before. I talk regularly with my therapist. It is so helpful to speak with someone who is neutral to my situation and who can hear me out, but also help me understand and communicate better with my husband and others. If I can learn to communicate better inside his office, I can communicate better outside the office too.

"In therapy, I have learned a lot about myself which has helped. I used to say that my family drove me crazy. Now, I am beginning to see that maybe I was driving them crazy. I was too protective toward my children. How much protection do they need? I realized that maybe all my protection was really keeping them children and not letting them grow up. I was always trying to change my husband and pushing him to talk. My husband is a very private person. He is five years older than me. I had unrealistic expectations. He is a different person and has different needs. He was raised in a different home with different parents. I have to tell him what I want. I'm beginning to understand that what I really wanted from him was affection and support. He cannot read my mind. Now I ask him to give me a hug when I feel stressed. This was Dr. Zal's suggestion. He is more than willing to do it and it really helps. Recently, he lost his job. I immediately tried to fix it and make a plan. If we have a plan, we will be okay. He said, 'Let me be a man and let me handle it.' I've started to realize that I try to be in charge and try to fix everything. My being in charge prevents me from getting anxious. It's okay if other people help."

My Opinion of What Helped Andrea's Anxiety

In the beginning of our sessions together, Andrea and I just talked. I wanted to understand her more and see how she saw the people in her life. I wanted to understand what was making her feel so negative. Overall, she was very frustrated and angry because she felt that she had to carry the entire world (at home and at work) on her shoulders. It brought back memories of when she was seven and her father went to prison, leaving her in charge. She began to see how she contributed to her present situation and she started to make some changes in her behavior and lifestyle.

Andrea was right: She did have a problem with trust and communication with those that she loved. However, after a few sessions, it became apparent that Andrea's main difficulty was that she suffered from GAD, the symptoms of which had been escalating as her frustration with herself and others increased. I started her on an antianxiety prescription and the medication was helpful. After two weeks on this medication, she reported that she was mulling things over less, had more patience, was sleeping better and had increased energy. I also taught her the deep breathing exercise, which helped her pause and refocus.

As we discussed her issues in our sessions, it became apparent to Andrea that although she saw herself as this very independent person, she also had dependency needs and wanted support from others. It took her a long time to finally share information about her father. She told me that when her father left for prison, he charged her (his only child) with the responsibility of protecting her mom. He worried that people would take advantage of his wife. Andrea admitted that she spoke to her mother several times a day to check up on her. I asked her, "What do you gain from this behavior?"

She responded, "When I'm anxious and on the crazy train, I call her." She became tearful and continued, "I don't know what I would do if she wasn't around. I've always been comforted by my mom."

I wondered out loud, "Who is taking care of whom?" She started to understand that her relationship with her mother gave her a lot of the support that she needed. Even independent people need support at times, someone to lean on for emotional security, when they are feeling low or frazzled. It is not a sign of weakness to lean on others at times. We all have many complex facets to our personalities and sometimes even seemingly contradictory needs.

We also discussed Eric Berne's transactional analysis theory of communication. People can relate as parent/child, child/parent or more effectively as adult/adult.[4] Andrea often communicated as parent to child and then was surprised when she elicited childish responses from others. These characteristic ways of relating can be changed. By using Berne's reference points she started to understand what was going on in some of her communications with her husband, children and others. It helped her interact in a more adult manner. In therapy she initially put me on a pedestal and made me the all-knowing adult. She often referred to my suggestions as "homework." I pointed out that I was not her school teacher, her priest, her father or a judge. She tried to relate to me on a more "adult-to-adult" level.

I was not surprised that, when Andrea changed her behavior, her husband also changed. Some clients will ask me, "Why do I have to come to see you? He or she is the problem; why don't they come?" I offer to see them both together, if the other partner will come for marital therapy. However, I tell my clients with marital or relationship problems that most couples are like a seesaw. A couple, like two people on this piece of playground equipment, must maintain equilibrium between them. Even if only one of them comes for therapy, there can still be positive results in the relationship. When one changes his or her behavior, the other must also change so that the couple's equilibrium on the relationship seesaw can stay balanced.

We focused on the issue of acceptance of self and others. Interpersonal relationships are not always easy. You can only take responsibility for your own actions and your half of the interaction. We all have good and bad points. If you expect yourself and everyone else to be perfect, you will always be frustrated. Have realistic expectations of yourself and others. All people want to be accepted for who they are: being a whole person includes the positive and the negative. You cannot change other people even though many marry hoping that they will be able to change their spouse or significant other. This cannot be done and can cause much frustration in a relationship. Most people do grow and change, but some never do.

Make peace with who you are and believe in yourself. Accept your limitations. There are many things that are not under your control. I told Andrea that adult children, for instance, often give their parents higher marks on parenting than the parents might give themselves.

Another issue that contributed to Andrea's frustration was her need to be the caregiver and take care of everyone else. Anxious people, particularly those with traumatic backgrounds, tend to like to be in charge. This allows them to feel more in control and less vulnerable. However, at times this backfires, particularly during times in their lives when they themselves need support. Sometimes the people whom they have chosen are not capable of giving them what they need and often they do not ask for what they want. Pride and fear of rejection stand in the way. Verbalize your feelings, concerns and needs as directly as you can, but don't hit people over the head with your feelings and blame others. Fortunately, Andrea's husband was an adult who, when she learned to ask him for what she really wanted, was able to listen to her and give her that support.

In therapy we also discussed Andrea's problems in her relationship with her daughter, Jackie. Andrea's personality and background made her over-protective toward her teenage daughter, who was trying to branch out on her own. Andrea's tendency to worry combined with her own problems during adolescence made her more fearful for Jackie. At times, it made it harder for Andrea to let go and give her daughter room to grow. By description, Jackie seemed like an average teenage college student who was working part-time and doing well. I tried to explain to Andrea that the job of a teenager is to separate from his or her parents. If the teenager didn't, he or she would not mature. I posed the following questions and got these answers back from Andrea: Did Jackie take drugs? No. Was she in school? Yes. Was she working part time? Yes. Did she help a little around the house? Yes. Did she have friends? Yes. It all sounds good. Then, don't worry so much about her. Just be there for her if she needs you.

As we have seen before, anxious people like Andrea are often perfectionists, with high expectations of themselves and others. Anything less than 100 percent is seen as failure. This need for perfection often triggers the cycle of anxiety. This is what happened to Andrea when she got promoted at her workplace. Fearful of failing, she was often too immobilized to even start a task. I tried to get Andrea to understand that it would take time and that she had the ability. I told her that it would be helpful if she placed the emphasis on just doing a good job and having fun while trying, rather than on being the best and trying to please everyone. I shared Henry Ford's words with her: "Nothing is particularly hard if you divide it into small jobs."[5] Many like Andrea need frequent reassurance, particularly during the learning curve created by a new situation.

Although it took Andrea a long time to trust me enough to share some of her secrets, therapy proved very helpful for her. Venting her emotional pain alone was useful. However, she was also able to gain good insight, which allowed her to develop new coping mechanisms and a better emotional balance between dependence and independence. Her relationships at home and at work improved. Andrea was able to recognize the fact that she was and would always be an anxious person, but she realized that it was not a terrible thing or something that she had to hide. Andrea started to accept herself and others as human beings with good and bad points. She tried to have more reasonable expectations of herself and others and started to relate more adult-to-adult.

Andrea is more content now and even feels happy at times.

Chapter 10

Step 10:
Take Care of Yourself

Give yourself time and permission to relax. Be good to yourself. Take care of your body and your health. Exercise regularly and watch your diet. Avoid excessive caffeine and alcohol intake. Reduce salt intake. Keep away from nicotine and street drugs. Pay attention to personal relationships. Have symmetry each day between work and play. Balance is the key to leading a successful and fulfilled life.

Balance! This is the magic word that best describes how to lead a successful, content, fulfilled life and help calm your anxieties. Taking care of yourself involves many aspects. First is the physical part which involves your body, diet and exercise. Pay attention to nutrition and rest, watch your diet and keep your weight down. Get medical treatment early before physical problems escalate, see your doctor for a checkup at least once a year and get your required vaccinations, blood tests and age-appropriate medical tests. The next aspect to look at is your emotional perspective. People today work long hours and come home tired. Some of us marry and have children who keep us busy in so many ways. We run from here to there and seek gratification in material rewards. When does the fun begin? When does our real life begin? If we are lucky, one day we wake up and start to look at the whole picture. We realize that this is not a dress rehearsal. This minute, this hour, this day is our life. Enjoy it. Remember, it is all right to slow down a little and leave time for relaxation and fun.

Try to find meaningful work and goals that you like. These will give you a reason to get out of bed in the morning and look forward to the day ahead. See the complete picture, broaden your horizons and add new and interesting bricks to your foundation. Have your own life and don't rely on others to make you happy. That is not their job. Pay attention to the quality of your life. Develop interests and friendships that are meaningful to you, increase your level of intimacy in interpersonal relationships, get a hobby and perhaps do volunteer work. If we are lucky, we learn the lesson of love and its central position in a life of meaning. Don't forget to tell your spouse, children, significant other and friends that you love and appreciate them. We all welcome positive reinforcement.

The goal of psychiatric treatment is to reduce or alleviate your symptoms that interfere with functioning. It also can help you achieve maximum emotional and behavioral maturity and live up to your full potential. All theories of personality talk about helping the client to achieve growth and expand his or her horizons. This involves guiding the client toward a more independent and responsible lifestyle. One of the most gratifying aspects of being a psychiatrist is seeing a client grow emotionally, thrive and achieve success. I was delighted recently to learn that Bill, a client of mine with attention deficit disorder, had been accepted to Harvard Business School. I was also gratified to learn that Tom, another client of mine with a history of anxiety and low self-esteem, had been promoted to a national position at a large corporation. Next let's look at Jack, an anxious young man with great potential, as he travels from adolescence to adulthood, starts to mature, take care of himself and achieve better balance in his life.

Jack's Story

"My anxiety is exhausting, disturbing and wears me out. Even my friends call me 'Nervous Jack.' It manifests itself in different ways. It encompasses everything that I do. I can wake up in the morning feeling anxious and afraid to start the new day. I can have an anxiety

attack at lunch or have difficulty falling asleep, because I am over-
thinking events and what will happen tomorrow. Overall, though, it
presents itself through avoidance and self-sabotage. I give up if I'm not
the best. I can guarantee failure; success is a risk. The fear of failure
pushes me to stop trying, because then I can't let people down, myself
included. If I have no expectations of myself to begin with, I cannot
fall short. Whether it is a romantic or educational endeavor, you can
bet my anxiety will convince me that I have failed long before I even
start. Whether it is applying for a new job or looking for a new apart-
ment, guaranteed, I will have found an excuse as to why it won't work
out before I even start my computer to go online. While the intensity
of the anxiety fluctuates, the one constant is that it is always there;
whether or not I allow it to affect me is the difference."

Wearing jeans, a T-shirt and sneakers, Jack looked younger than his twenty-one years. Sitting hunched over, with his arms on his knees, he told me that three years ago he had experienced two seizures while living in a college dormitory. Although they never recurred, he was embarrassed, frightened, overwhelmed and felt out of control. He also felt guilty about how he had handled it. He'd increased his drinking and slowly stopped going to classes. He'd experimented with marijuana, cocaine, ecstasy and angel dust. His weight decreased to one hundred and twenty pounds on his six foot frame. "I was withering away," he said.

Jack often felt angry and agitated. A year later, he ended up breaking his hand when he punched his fist through a wall and was "kicked out of the dorm" and eventually left school. During this time, his grandmother and great aunt were killed in a car accident. Because these two people had been close to him and were part of his support system, this was a big loss for him. These deaths affected his parents negatively and therefore also impinged more on him and made him feel more alone. Jack had become an emergency medical technician (EMT) during one of his school co-op programs and therefore was able to get a job as part of an ambulance transport team. He was in turmoil as to what to do with the rest of his life.

During our first session, Jack reported that he had been depressed for the last two months since he completely stopped drinking alcohol. I was not surprised to hear this, because alcohol is a depressant. Moderate drinking may relax you initially and make you feel somewhat more peaceful, but heavy drinking often contributes to or causes depression and increased anxiety in the long run, because alcohol influences the brain in ways similar to anxiety and depression. A person who has an emotional or psychiatric problem plus an alcohol or drug problem is defined as having a "dual diagnosis." Depression and anxiety disorders are among the common mental health problems that coexist with alcohol or drug abuse.

Jack's weight had ballooned up to two hundred and twelve pounds. His energy was diminished, he had difficulty falling and staying asleep and he was ruminative and tended to overthink everything. When I questioned him, he denied suicidal thoughts and exclaimed, "I want to live!" He was anxious, avoidant and felt on edge, irritable and restless. He complained of vague physical distress, particularly muscle tension in his chest and stomach pains. He had a history of panic attacks that involved palpitations, tunnel vision, everything going black and feeling as if he was going to die. "I freeze up, don't know what to do and feel inadequate," he said. He told me that in mid-adolescence, he had been treated for attention deficit disorder (ADD) with various stimulant medications. In passing, almost as an afterthought, he also mentioned that his father had recently been diagnosed with duodenal cancer.

It seemed to me that Jack had been crying out for help for some time. I suspected that he had been chronically mildly depressed and had felt inadequate, lost and alone for a while. His initial interview gave me multiple diagnostic clues and made me entertain possible diagnoses including GAD, panic disorder, major depressive disorder, ADD, alcohol dependency in remission, polysubstance abuse in remission, perhaps post-traumatic stress disorder or bipolar II disorder. I decided to start with what seemed to be bothering him the most, which was his sense of being overwhelmed and anxious. Although he had been experiencing much adolescent confusion, he seemed more solid than he thought.

I asked him to describe his parents, because I was hopeful that under-standing how he saw them would allow me to understand him better. He said: "My mother is anxious and a worrier. She is affectionate, laid back and shy but can also be outgoing. She has a sense of humor and is compassionate. When I was young, she came to me for advice. She raised me too fast. I always had to be the peacemaker in the house. I was always an 'old soul.' She didn't get angry; instead, she got sad. She was the queen of the guilt trip. She had tried various occupations from business to health sciences."

I particularly wanted to hear about his relationship with his father. I suspected that it played a role in his present condition. A physically present and engaged father can be a positive role model in the life of his son. He shared only the following, "My father, a police officer, is also anxious. I was raised strictly. He could be affectionate, outgoing and funny, but he had a short temper and could yell and scream." Jack felt that his parents were over-protective but that they both loved him.

This description of how Jack perceived his parents and his self-analysis showed me that he was struggling to define and clarify some of these same personality traits in himself. At age twenty-one, he was still going through adolescent turmoil trying to decide who he was. When I asked him to list his good and bad points, he said, "My good points are that I have a sense of humor, am creative, caring and like to help people. My bad points are that I am anxious, shy and insecure. I have a fear of commitment and like to set myself up for failure…when I got angry, I used to punch walls. Now, I sometimes drink, yell a lot and run off." He admitted that taking care of others gave him a feeling of closeness to people, helped him feel in charge and allowed him to ignore his own problems.

Like many others, Jack's bravado and his leadership pose covered up feelings of inadequacy. Low self-esteem is one of the major recurring themes that I deal with in psychotherapy. Regardless of their initial complaints, weak self-worth is a river that runs through the land of angst where many clients live. Negative feelings and distorted perspectives on themselves eclipse their true potential. Many times, poor self-esteem goes back to messages received in childhood. In therapy, I try to give a more positive and balanced point of view. To help them truly grow, I must improve how clients feel about themselves. Sometimes, it takes nothing more than giving them a legitimate compliment or pointing out how well they are doing in a particular area. When I do this, I can almost see the inner glow that the praise produces.

Another client of mine, Neil, expressed his own similarity to Jack's plight when he wrote, "My anxiety is not feeling adequate, feeling threatened about the circumstances around me, feeling like things aren't going to work out, feeling like I'm disappointing a family member or that I'm going to be abandoned. Anxiety is feeling more upset about the present and future than thankful about the past. Anxiety is not trusting in God to supply all of my needs. Anxiety is worrying that my children aren't going to use their potential to the fullest or miss an opportunity to do their best." Although there are differences between Neil and Jack, there are also many parallels that come up frequently with anxious people.

At times, Jack spoke about his relationships with "girls." He seemed to need to have a girlfriend in his life at all times. "I like broke girls who I can try to fix," he said. His choices seemed to verify this statement. His first love, whom he dated between ages fourteen and fifteen, "had a mental breakdown." His next choice as a girlfriend became a "drama fest with a lot of bickering and verbal fighting. It was all mind games." At eighteen, he found that his latest girlfriend was sleeping with all of his friends. His need to take care of others extended to his male friends as well. Several years before, his best friend had become a heroin addict and subsequently had died of an overdose. "I had tried hard to be there for him," Jack said. "It was a shock. I felt guilty. I take on the whole world's problems…I'm pissed, because we all tried to help him." During our therapy time, another of Jack's friends died of suicide by drug overdose. Jack dealt with it by punching a hole in the wall. These losses gave us a chance to talk about how he dealt with anger and feeling helpless. They allowed us to discuss his cycle of inadequacy, anger, guilt and sadness.

Much of his turmoil had to do with his future in reference to school and occupational direction. This is a common problem with young people in their late teens and early twenties. "I can't sleep," he said. "I'm thinking about the future. Should I be a police officer, a firefighter, a special education teacher or go into medicine? My fantasy is of me helping people and saving someone's life." One of Jack's greatest roadblocks to advancement was his anxiety and his tendency to worry. Anxiety prevented him from taking risks and leaving his comfort zone. His worries reinforced his uncertainties and his dread of the unknown: "I'm fearful that I will have another seizure." Having a seizure would be the ultimate loss of control for Jack. He also worried about other aspects of his health, often complaining of vague feelings of chest tightness and heartburn. "I wish that I could get paid for my worry," he said. "I would be a millionaire. I worry about stupid stuff that doesn't even matter."

After much rumination and angst, Jack gradually found some direction. He signed up for paramedic school to get his associate's degree in emergency medical science. He got ready by taking math and English courses online and anatomy and physiology classes during the summer at a community college. His two year stint in paramedic school was a constant battle of wills. Luckily, his teacher saw his potential and offered constant support. At one point, Jack flunked an examination and wanted to quit. The teacher was sure that Jack knew the material and insisted that he retake the examination. When my children were young and became anxious about an exam or other life event, my wife would tell them that they needed two calm elephants, one on each side, to give them a sense of security and help them feel calm. My wife and I were the calm elephants for our children. Similarly, this teacher and I were Jack's two calm mentors and helped motivate him toward the graduation finish line.

Jack's Opinion of What Helped His Anxiety

"When I was younger, I used to think drinking helped my anxiety. I found out that this was a lie. At first, it relaxed me and let me have fun when I was a teenager. In the long run, as Dr. Zal taught me, it is really a depressant chemically and will just increase my depression.

"Personally, I feel that just getting up in the morning, going out and doing it has helped the most. Dr. Zal kept telling me 'avoid avoidance.' It helped me finish school, even when every part of me swore I was going to fail, swore that I wasn't going to make it, swore that I should just quit. I kept telling myself, 'Stay strong. Don't go down the anxiety rabbit hole. Everything will be all right.' Now, I distract myself with work. I call this 'tactful avoidance.'

"A structured environment helps me as well; this is funny, because I have chosen a career path that finds traditional schedules non-existent. The more active I remain, the less time I have to get stuck in my own head and the less my anxiety builds up. It's almost as if by keeping myself moderately busy, I'm preventing the pot from boiling over. Overall, I would say simple conversations with Dr. Zal are what keep it in check the most. Dr. Zal calls me out on my bullshit and helps me connect the logical and emotional parts of my brain. These two aspects of me are constantly ignoring each other. I now realize that I used to play to my imaginary audience. I did things to please others. I had to grow up too soon. My mother used me as her confidante. My father, the cop, encouraged me to be a leader and be in control. That's how my need for control began. I grew up quickly behaviorally, but I am still growing emotionally. I don't blame them. I now know that they love me and they did their best.

"Support and encouragement from my parents, my teachers and Dr. Zal helped a lot. When I first met Dr. Zal, I didn't know if therapy would work. The first two times we got together, I said to myself, 'he's not buying into my deflection plays.' I had always played mental chess with therapists before and it wasn't working here. Now, sitting outside by the fire on the patio at my parent's house, relaxing and sometimes talking to my father is helpful. When I was younger, I never knew who I was going to get when my father was around. He was taking pain meds for a chronic shoulder injury. Sometimes he was in a bad mood, asleep or loopy. Where was he when I needed him? Now, I have a coherent dad. We are building a better relationship. We talk and he gives me life advice. We go to Phillies games together."

I was glad to hear about the improvement in their father-son relationship. I had felt for a long time that one of the reasons that Jack wanted to be in therapy was that he needed a male mentor to occasionally offer guidance and reassurance during rough spots along the road. Adolescents, trying to be autonomous and break their dependent bonds with their parents, may reject their mothers and fathers. However, there are times that it is still helpful to have parents in their lives. Jack's father's health problems and the deaths in the family had caused him to withdraw from Jack. It created a void that may have been interpreted incorrectly by Jack as meaning that his father didn't care about him. This feeling of loss and abandonment can contribute to anger and rage. As Jack's relationship with his father healed and improved and his life seemed to be more fulfilling, he started coming to therapy less often.

My Opinion of What Helped Jack's Anxiety

Growing up with Jack again in the therapy room by asking him questions about his childhood and adolescence allowed me to help him gain some insight into how he became the man he was. He was able to use this insight to change his behavior. Jack was a "sickly child." Due to physical problems (frequent bouts of strep throat, broken bones, tonsillitis), Jack was often out of school and missed out on interacting with other children his age. His physical problems left him feeling weak, helpless, inadequate and fearful of bodily illness. He would often say, "I always feel broken. I'm a lemon." Health issues, combined with ADD problems and his innate anxiety, slowed down his interpersonal skills development with other children. These two factors, along with his low self-esteem, left him feeling more comfortable being the leader rather than a follower. He explained it well when he said, "I define myself by my work. I feel the most comfortable in my job uniform. On the job, I have total control; I know just what I have to do. My anxiety goes out the window." Any subsequent stressors in his life that involved health issues or bodily injury caused him to regress emotionally and once again feel inadequate, out of control and "broken."

I tried to bolster Jack's self-esteem by pointing out his positive traits and abilities. I told him not to compare himself and his achievements to people who were older than himself. I would ask him, "How are you doing compared to other twenty-one-year-olds?" I refused to allow him to be negative and put himself down.

Last summer he volunteered to be a counselor for eight to twelve-year-olds at a camp for children with seizure disorders run by the regional epilepsy foundation. This position gave him a new perspective and helped him reduce his anxiety about his seizure disorder: "I saw these kids having frequent seizures and I realized that my situation was not so bad." He was looking forward to working there again. The professional group leaders really seemed to like him and asked him to start a youth council for them. They also sent him to California for three days to represent the foundation at a leadership and skill-building conference. He had a great time and felt accepted, which did much to increase his feelings of self-esteem and his self-confidence.

Overprotected as a child, he identified with the parental role and wanted to take care of others. He also wanted a woman in his life to take care of him and make him feel safe and secure. This scenario played out again when Jack was doing his EMT preparation. He got involved with a young woman who kept pushing herself into his life. Busy with school and work, he liked having a woman in his life but he finally realized that he was using her, didn't love her and could stand on his own without a security blanket. With much trepidation, he broke the relationship off.

He also put a lot of pressure on himself to please his parents and other authority figures, because without them in his corner he felt vulnerable and helpless. He felt that if he disappointed them they might not be there to take care of him. Jack once said, "When my mother dies, I will be in here every day." I knew we had a lot to talk about concerning his dependency needs.

Jack overcompensated by overworking, because at work he felt most comfortable and most in control. He had three jobs: an ambulance EMT, a teacher of cardio-pulmonary resuscitation (CPR) at a medical school and an EMT for a national event services company. I called him twice to check various chronological details and both times he couldn't talk, because he was working. One of the biggest things that I tried to get across to Jack was the importance of balance in his life. We all have a need for balance between work and play to help reduce stress, nurture and sustain us. If you have two plants, one representing work and the other representing the rest of your life (relationships, hobbies, play) and you only water and take care of the work plant, it will grow and the other will not. I encouraged Jack to water his lifestyle plant by spending time relaxing, exercising, taking care of himself, being with his friends and developing other non-work interests. I explained to him that this was not selfishness, but rather self-preservation.

I knew something had changed when Jack came in one day and he had cut his long hair—he looked more his age. He started to lose weight and went for several job interviews. He was offered—and took—a job as a paramedic associated with a regional trauma center. He also kept working part time covering special events. He even made an appointment with a neurologist to see what he should do about his seizure medication. He quit smoking. Unfortunately, in spite of his progress, Jack's anxiety still colored and defined his perspective. During a later session he said, "I'm nervous that I'm doing better. I'm afraid that something bad will happen." Nevertheless, he gradually spent more time with his friends and family. He started taking one weekend off a month just for himself. He started going to a gym and made time for his volunteer work at the epilepsy foundation.

Recently he walked in in a positive mood, standing straight and tall, and happily announced, "I don't feel crazy anymore. I see people whom I take care of at work who are a lot worse. I realize now that I mistook [poor] coping skills, adolescent rebellion and confidence issues for mental instability."

"Nervous Jack" was moving forward, conquering tasks and his own anxiety one day at a time. He was feeling better about himself and taking care of himself. He was looking at the whole picture and trying to maintain a balance in his life. He seemed more content. He was moving on down the road to maturity and full adulthood. I couldn't have been more proud.

Part II

Treatment Options

Chapter 11

Therapy

When I first started in my solo practice of psychiatry more than forty years ago, the treatment options that I could offer were limited. During my fellowship in psychiatry I had been trained to do psychoanalytically-oriented individual and group psychotherapy. My job was to listen carefully and empathetically to clients' stories and ask questions about their early years, including their childhoods and adolescences. I would ask them to describe their parents or others who raised them. My goal was to grow up with them again to see how they had become the people they were. I could make a diagnosis and offer education and reassurance. Otherwise, I was to remain a blank screen upon which the clients could play out their internal conflicts and subsequently gain insight.

During my psychiatric training, I was taught to concern myself with such issues as transference (the displacement of patterns of feelings and behaviors originally experienced with significant figures of one's childhood to individuals in one's current relationships) and countertransference (the partially unconscious attitudes and feelings of the therapist toward the client).[1] Although I believe in the basic Freudian tenets underlying insight-oriented psychotherapy and still use this framework when doing therapy today, I soon grew weary of the limited interaction with clients and gradually grew more eclectic in my choice of treatment methods. My clients appreciated a therapist who talked to them more and seemed to do better with this new approach.

Through the years, treatment choices for therapy and medications useful for the treatment of anxiety have increased tremendously. Today we have many options available to help. I believe that GAD responds best to a holistic approach. I use a combination of education about the disorder to foster reassurance and acceptance, psychotherapy to gain a new perspective, behavioral techniques to modulate the anxiety response and psychopharmacology, where appropriate, to reduce the emotional and physical symptoms of anxiety. The client vignettes that appear throughout the book illustrate that my clients often brought in their own treatment choices and suggestions. I am not against anything that helps, as long as it causes no harm. However, in this day of effective psychiatric medications, I feel that the combination of pharmacology and some form of psychotherapy produces the greatest benefit for most clients with chronic anxiety. Psychiatrists can now offer or recommend these therapies and treatments:

Education, Reassurance and Acceptance
    Psychotherapy
    Group Psychotherapy
    Cognitive-behavioral Therapy (CBT)

Behavioral Relaxation Techniques
    Progressive Muscle Relaxation (PMR)
    Deep Breathing
    Visualization, Guided Imagery, Affirmation
    Meditation
    Yoga
    Mindfulness
    Self-hypnosis
    Biofeedback
    Massage Therapy

Lifestyle Changes
    Exercise, Diet, etc.
    Spirituality and Religion

Pharmacology
    Medications, Herbal Remedies

Education, Reassurance and Acceptance

You may have many fears and fantasies about what is wrong with you and what your symptoms mean. A clear understanding of anxiety, including its meaning and an explanation of where it comes from, hopefully will mitigate most of your fears that you have a physical illness or a brain tumor or are going crazy. Be reassured that anxiety symptoms are not a sign of weakness, failure or childishness. They are not anyone's fault. You do not have to feel guilty or punish yourself. Remember also that although anxiety can be very uncomfortable and frightening, no one ever dies from anxiety alone. All of your negative thoughts such as, "I am going to lose control, go crazy or die," really mean, "I am feeling anxious."

Starting to gain acceptance is also a part of the initial phase of treatment. Anxiety is a biological illness that studies show can be inherited. You probably were predetermined to develop anxiety and worry due to a genetic vulnerability. It is an innate response which has been reinforced through the years. Anxiety-prone individuals such as you probably will never become 100 percent laid back and completely calm. Therapy will not make you a different person inside and out. A more realistic goal is that treatment can reduce the level of current anxiety, keep anxiety from escalating, modulate future symptomatic responses and increase your ability to cope and function more effectively. Remember, anxiety is not all negative. In moderate degrees, it does have some positive aspects. It can serve as a biological warning system that is activated during times of potential danger or threat. It can allow you to do your best in preparing for various challenging activities by increasing alertness and effort. It can be conducive to learning and growth.

However, in spite of this information, many with GAD are frustrated by their anxiety. David, one of my clients, explained it well when he said, "Anxiety is frustrating. It controls me because I live in constant fear of it. My biggest fear is that I do not know when it is going to hit me. I fear feeling anxious in public and people noticing that I'm having an issue. I would be embarrassed. It frustrates me that I do not always understand my anxiety. Why does it usually happen at work and around people I know well, like friends and co-workers? Also, why do I feel great one day and then the next day the anxiety can hit me again? My biggest frustration is that I cannot control my feelings and I get down on myself that I can't get past it. I know that I overthink it, but I still find myself unable to stop these moods." Clients like this need continued reassurance and therapy to put their frustrations in perspective, change their thought patterns and quell their apprehension. Let's look more closely at some of the therapies that are available.

Psychotherapy

In my opinion, psychotherapy is the keystone to helping people reduce their anxiety and use their new energies more constructively to learn to relax and enjoy life. In spite of psychopharmacological progress, the need for human contact remains constant, particularly when we are feeling stressed and needy. In this day of "medication management," where psychiatrists are often marginalized and insurance companies assign therapy cases to psychologists, I feel it is so important to emphasize my firm belief that although psychiatric medications can facilitate improvement, it is people working with people on a sustained, long-term basis that is equally—or even more— important in maintaining recovery. The therapist-client relationship is a powerful therapeutic force. Sebastian Zimmerman, M.D., in his article, "Intimate Portraits: Psychotherapists in Their Own Work Space," emphasizes this point when he says: "Psychotherapy can change the brain. The catalyst for change lies in the relationship between the client and the therapist. In my own experience as a psychiatrist, therapy has not only clinical—but also poetic and magical—moments."[2]

Establishing rapport and transmitting empathetic concern is essential to effective treatment. You may have to shop around until you find a therapist who listens to you with compassion and acceptance and with whom you feel comfortable. Although credentials may be similar, personalities and "bedside manners" differ. It is often difficult today to find a psychiatrist who can offer both therapy and medication management. A 2012 study by the American Psychiatric Institute for Research and Education explains that there is a "lost generation" of young psychiatrists who were trained to do only medication management. Psychiatrists who predominantly provide psychotherapy tend to be over the age of sixty-five. The study recommends that, since there is evidence that psychotherapy is an effective biological treatment, it once again be included in psychiatric residency training.[3]

Individual or group psychotherapy can provide either insight or support focus, depending on your ability to interact therapeutically and your capacity for introspection. I find that a combined approach is effective for most people. All types of therapy have certain general goals: teaching coping skills, helping boost self-confidence and encouraging a feeling of increased control. Therapy needs to promote emotional growth, a more adult point of view and realistic expectations of people and situations. It can allow people to talk and release feelings, place things in perspective and encourage goal-directed behavior. In life, as in art and photography, perspective changes everything. Marcel Proust said, "The real voyage of discovery consists not in seeking new lands, but in seeing with new eyes."[4]

In psychoanalytical or insight-oriented psychotherapy, anxiety is seen as a signal that the defenses or coping mechanisms used to protect the ego (the self) are collapsing due to internal threats from forbidden (but instinctual) sexual or aggressive drives, which causes "neurotic" conflict. The therapist needs to ask him or herself two questions: "What inner drivers is the client afraid of?" and "What are the consequences that he or she fears will follow their expression?" This type of psychotherapy will provide understanding of emotional conflicts, the unconscious meaning of anxiety, the possible symbolism of the avoided situation, the need to repress impulses and the advantages derived from the symptoms. With this type of therapy, I often say that I have to peel back one layer of the onion at a time to slowly resolve the "neurotic" conflict of the feelings of fear, guilt or anger that keeps the client from doing what he or she really wants to do.

If the problem is narrower in focus and more related to the external world, a supportive therapeutic approach may be effective to reduce conflict, relieve symptoms and encourage progress. This type of therapy offers an opportunity for ventilation and a chance to tease out hidden stressors in a comfortable and accepting environment. In the course of reducing anxiety, new gains can be obtained in exploring emotional needs, increasing comfort with personal feelings and moving toward a more independent and responsible lifestyle.

People often ask why therapy can be so tiring. The answer is that the therapist, regardless of the type of therapy practiced, is doing active listening. That takes focused energy and can be wearing.

Group Psychotherapy

Group psychotherapy started in America as a medical experiment in 1906 when J.H. Pratt, a Boston physician, held classes at home for tuberculosis patients.[5] The group setting can be helpful for GAD clients. Here they can share their experiences and problems and learn that they are not alone or "different." Here they will feel less isolated and begin to realize that they have a specific, understandable syndrome and not a bizarre condition. In group, they can experience a decrease in anxiety, obtain relief from guilty feelings and achieve an increase in self-esteem, because they are being taken seriously. Group therapy can foster self-expression and ventilation, as well as better interpersonal relationships and communication.

My own group style is a combination of teaching communication skills and using the psychoanalytic model to examine the needs of the individual as they emerge in response to the interaction of the group. Here anxiety clients are taught to look at their own and others' feelings, to listen to other people, to give feedback on how they feel and to examine their assumptions. Through group work in building cohesiveness, the client and the group will gain strength. As group members grapple with the fantasy that the therapist will cure them, they deal with their own dependency needs. Finally, the group process helps bring into focus transference and resistance phenomena (your opposition to anything that disturbs your inner psychic balance) that can then be analyzed in individual sessions.

Cognitive-Behavioral Therapy (CBT)

This is a method to understand how thoughts and feelings influence behavior. It is based on the idea that it is our thoughts, not external things like people, situations and events, that cause our behaviors. The benefit of this is that we can change the way we think and act even if the situation does not change. During the course of treatment, you will learn how to identify and change destructive or disturbing thought patterns that have negative influences on your behavior. Author Robert Fulghum illustrates this premise when he says, "People, places and events are panic-provoking only after we apply meaning to them. A store is just a store, a speech is just a speech, a drive is just a drive, until our brains interpret them as 'dangerous' or 'threatening.'"[6] Cognitive-behavioral therapy is generally short term and focused on helping you deal with a very specific problem.

Cognitive Therapy

This corrects distorted ways of thinking (cognitive distortion). It can deal with the way that you think about yourself, what happens in your life and what you feel may happen in the future. It will attack your tendency to perceive danger based on false and negative premises. Anxious people tend to catastrophize, overestimate the likelihood of negative events and underestimate their ability to cope. They are prone to black and white thinking. Cognitive therapy stops the cycle of fear from escalating and will help you understand that these negative thoughts are just your mind's way of telling you that you are feeling anxious. By helping you become aware of inaccurate or negative thinking, cognitive therapy allows you to view challenging situations more clearly and respond to them in a more effective way. Here is what you will be asked to do:

1. Identify situations that trouble or worry you. These may include such things as financial issues, family matters, a medical condition, grief, anger or symptoms of a specific mental illness. You and your therapist will spend time prioritizing and deciding what problems and goals to work on.

2. Become aware of your thoughts, emotions and beliefs about these situations. Your therapist will encourage you to share your thoughts about them. This may include observing what you tell yourself about a possible outcome of an action or experience, your interpretation of the meaning of a situation and your beliefs about yourself, other people and events. Your therapist may suggest that you keep a journal of such thoughts.

3. Identify negative or inaccurate thinking. To help you recognize patterns of thinking and behavior that may be contributing to your problem, your therapist may ask you to pay attention to your physical, emotional and behavioral responses in different situations.

4. Challenge negative or inaccurate thinking. This will encourage you to test the validity of your thoughts and beliefs. It may include asking yourself whether your view of a situation is based on fact or based on an inaccurate perception of what's going on. This step can be difficult. You may have long-standing ways of thinking about your life and yourself. Many thought patterns are first developed in childhood. Thoughts and beliefs that you've held for a long time feel normal and correct, so it can be a challenge to recognize inaccuracies or negative tendencies in your thinking. With practice, helpful thinking and behavior patterns will become a habit and won't take as much effort.

Behavioral Relaxation Techniques

Progressive muscle relaxation (PMR)

Lie down in a comfortable position. Close your eyes. Tense your muscles sequentially through various parts of the body for ten seconds and relax them for twenty seconds—hands, arms, shoulders, muscles in your upper back, front and back of neck, stomach and chest, buttocks, thighs, calves and feet. Tighten each muscle group and then relax the muscles. Let the tension flow out. The whole PMR session takes approximately thirty minutes. PMR instructions are available on tape for your use or you can make your own.

Deep Breathing

Breathe in slowly through your nose and fill your lungs completely with air. Pause and hold your breath for a moment. Exhale very slowly through pursed lips. This will lower your heart rate and help you relax. You can do this one to three times. People around you will not notice and you will feel calmer. It is the breathing out slowly that is the most important part of this exercise. Many people hyperventilate when they become anxious. This rapid breathing causes a decrease of carbon dioxide (CO_2), which upsets the body's acid balance and causes physical symptoms such as muscle spasms and contractures. The deep breathing exercise helps bring this balance back to normal. The same effect can be gained by breathing into a paper bag, where you rebreathe CO_2.

Visualization or Guided Imagery

This is a technique where one creates a mental image of a desired positive outcome and repeatedly plays that image in the mind. It is a focused daydream that can help you achieve a goal. Affirmations are positive thoughts repeated in your mind that can help reprogram negative beliefs and replace them with more helpful beliefs. For instance, the thought, "I am a special, good person," can replace the negative belief, "I am a mess." Visualizations and affirmations create new belief systems by replacing negative thought patterns with more effective ones that help you take constructive action.

Meditation

Meditation is a way to empty your mind of thoughts in order to relax and decrease anxiety. In the Hindu tradition of transcendental meditation, a mantra is used for relaxing and refreshing the mind and body through the repetition of a soothing word, phrase or sound. To do this, sit in a comfortable place or position. Close your eyes. Slowly repeat your mantra. Gradually allow your voice to get lower and lower each time that you say your mantra. If thoughts intrude, go back to your mantra. Continue for twenty minutes.

Judy, a client of mine, recently brought in information about Maum meditation, which was founded in 1996 by Woo Myung. *Maum* means the mind, soul and spirit in Korean. It is a guided method of subtraction that allows you to become free of the limitations imposed by your past which Myung believes is recorded and stored within your mind as pictures. These pictures dictate thoughts, emotions, desires, behaviors and health. Although these pictures are illusions, humans unknowingly live within the illusions in their mind, thinking that they are real. Practitioners of Maum meditation believe that by using this method you will throw away old thoughts, find unconditional happiness and live in a true reality where you will find peace and learn to appreciate life in a new way. It promises relief from stress, anxiety and worry.[7]

Yoga

A system of exercises for attaining bodily or mental control and well-being, yoga uses a series of poses that can be relaxing and anxiety reducing. It can also increase strength, flexibility and balance. A slow, patient approach is helpful. Do what you can. You will gradually improve. Many books can be helpful. Recorded yoga sessions and interactive videogames are available to help you with this technique. Classes at all levels are available in most cities.

Mindfulness

This stress-reduction strategy has become very popular in the last few years and is what we used to call "focusing on the here and now." It is a technique, borrowed from Buddhist practices, to help you slow down and overcome anxiety through mindful acceptance by immersing yourself in the present moment with full focus and awareness. It shifts your thinking away from your need for control and self-centeredness and puts you in a state of active attention on the present, where you are observing your thoughts and feelings from a distance without judging them as good or bad. It will help you accept your anxiety symptoms and take action to live with them more effectively. It will help decrease negative thoughts and self-criticism through teaching you acceptance and compassion. It will help you pull yourself out of the habit of worrying about the future, which can develop into anxiety. It will send a calming wave of relaxation through your body.

Learning to slow down, focus and live in the moment is difficult for people who are anxiety prone. However, you are not your thoughts and you will enjoy life more if you can center on the moment, really be present and enjoy time spent with your children, friends and other loved ones. You will gain more pleasure out of life's experiences if you can truly immerse yourself in them 100 percent without giving so much of your energy to your negative thoughts and other cognitive distortions.

Self-Hypnosis

With this technique to induce relaxation based on positive suggestion, you can learn how to control your thoughts and replace negative ones with pleasant ones. You can suggest to yourself that the problem at hand is not as bad as believed. There are many scripts that you can use. They all involve visualization and positive affirmations. Here is one that I suggest:

1. Find a quiet place where you can sit without being disturbed.

2. Close your eyes.

3. Breathe in, counting to six, and then breathe out, also counting to six. Imagine each inhalation as accepting the good. Imagine each exhalation as releasing anger and frustration.

4. Visualize yourself standing on a boardwalk. There are ten steps leading down to a beautiful beach. It is a sunny, gorgeous day with white clouds floating in a pale blue sky. Slowly, staying relaxed, walk down the steps onto the beach and sit down in a comfortable position. Affirm how you will solve your problem. Let the negative thoughts float up into the clouds and watch them slowly drift away.

5. Walk slowly back up the ten steps to the boardwalk. On each step reaffirm the positive outcome.

Biofeedback

Using devices to measure muscle tension and blood flow and giving a picture of your body's physiological state, this method teaches you to relax tense muscles. The Association for Applied Psychophysiology and Biofeedback, the Biofeedback Certification Institution of America and the International Society for Neurofeedback and Research arrived at a consensus definition of biofeedback in 2008. It states: "Biofeedback is a process that enables an individual to learn how to change physiological activity for the purposes of improving health and performance. Precise instruments measure physiological activity such as brainwaves, heart function, breathing, muscle activity and skin temperature. These instruments rapidly and accurately 'feed back' information to the user. The presentation of this information, often in conjunction with changes in thinking, emotions and behavior, supports desired physiological changes. Over time, these changes can endure without continued use of an instrument."[8]

Massage Therapy

Massage therapy can relieve muscle tension, foster relaxation and reduce stress. Although there are many types of relaxation massage, these are the most common: *Swedish massage* uses light to medium pressure. *Deep tissue massage* focuses on the underlying layer of muscles. *Reflexology* applies pressure to areas of the hands and feet called "reflex zones." It is based on the principle that there are reflexes in these areas that correspond to every part, organ and gland of the body. *Therapeutic massage* can be more specific for chronic complaints and injuries involving the joints, back and head and other medical problems. Included here is *sports massage* to manage pain and improve flexibility and range of motion.

Lifestyle Changes

Exercise

Move around every day. One of the best ways to deal with anxiety is exercise and physical movement. A physical workout is a wonderful way to relieve stress and dissipate tension. Scheduling a regular time to walk, play tennis, do aerobics or ride a bicycle not only allows you to step back from the anxiety of everyday life, but also encourages muscle relaxation and provides an escape from internal ruminations ("thinking, thinking, thinking") and worry.

Diet

Avoid excessive caffeine intake. Peter, a client of mine, had very high anxiety. In the past, therapy and medication had not brought him resolution. During my initial evaluation I questioned him about his caffeine intake and found that he was drinking eight to ten cups of regular coffee per day as well as a few caffeine-laden soft drinks. He felt that he needed them to "keep going" and do well at work. I asked him to start drinking half-decaffeinated coffee. Gradually, he was able to wean himself off caffeine and calmed down considerably. Brain receptors can be blocked by the caffeine in coffee, tea, chocolate and soft drinks. This inhibits the ability of the natural antianxiety substance GABA, produced by the body, to go into action. Reduce or stop alcohol and cigarette smoking. Halt the salt. Doing this will decrease fluid retention and thus help reduce blood pressure and put less strain on the heart.

Sleep

Avoiding fatigue and developing good sleep patterns is important. Make use of the rules for good sleep habits, such as: go to sleep and wake up at the same time each day, keep your bedroom uncluttered and calm, use your bed only for sleep and sex, avoid large meals just before bedtime, avoid stimulants such as caffeine products and ginseng before bedtime—instead drink a warm glass of milk—and avoid activities before bedtime that can stimulate your brain and make it difficult to get to sleep. These include vigorous physical exercise, computer-based activities and television shows that involve action or tension. Instead, do something relaxing before you go to sleep, such as taking a warm bath or shower or listening to soothing music. Keep a pad and pen on your nightstand. If you cannot fall asleep, because you are thinking about what you have to do the next day, write down your thoughts. The list will be there in the morning and your mind can stop running through your concerns. Avoid daytime sleeping. Chronic insomnia often overlaps with GAD.

Take Care of Medical Problems

See your family physician at least once a year for a physical exam and blood tests to rule out medical causes of anxiety, such as hypertension, hyperthyroidism and cardiac arrhythmias. If you are diabetic, be sure that your sugar levels are under control.

Expand Your Horizons

Anxious people lead hectic lives and feel that they have to do everything themselves. Finding a better balance in your life between yourself, your family, a significant other and work is important. I encourage you to reach out to others for friendship and support. Even strong people need support from others at times. An individualized treatment program for anxiety needs to include the encouragement of new hobbies and interests as a way to take your mind off of anxiety-producing problems and enlarge your support system.

Spirituality and Religion

The world is chaotic. Religion helps many by giving them something to hold on to during the chaos. It teaches acceptance, forgiveness and compassion for yourself and others. Rabbi Harold Kushner shares his philosophy in his book, *Conquering Fear: Living Boldly in an Uncertain World*. He says that God tells us "don't be afraid."[9] Kushner further states: "It all begins with gratitude and self-awareness, being thankful for who you are and what you have…face life without illusions. Face your problems and deal with them and you will discover that you are stronger than you think."[10] He says that he invokes God's presence, not to give God his problems, but to feel less alone, feel more hopeful, feel stronger and free himself to take effective action. He believes that prayer is one of the best ways to alleviate the sense of helplessness brought on by anxiety.[11]

These words of wisdom are taught by and hold true for many religious ideologies. All faiths promise a haven of calm within the doors of their sanctuaries. Here they offer rituals and services that can help alleviate anxiety, increase security and help you feel more in control. Religious leaders can serve as counselors at times of life crises or stress. Catholics go to confession and some pray daily to gain a sense of strength and balance in their lives. Muslims pray five times a day to reinforce their faith and receive similar positive feelings in return.

An anxious client of mine whose eldest son committed suicide told me that his faith helped him and his wife deal with this loss. He shared: "If everybody had a healthy dose of spirituality, it would be a better world. If you guide your life by religious tenets, you will be happier, healthier and have a positive mental outlook and treat your fellow man a lot better. Just go to church one hour a week."

Religion also allows us to be part of a larger community and helps us reduce the anxiety brought about by the isolating world that we live in today. Attending some form of worship, even occasionally, can offer emotional support and a feeling of connection as we get to know the clergy and the congregation. Religious traditions are a vital link between generations. Support them and lead by example. The warm feelings of family togetherness at holiday time or on other occasions are special moments. Share your positive childhood traditions with your children and encourage them to start new traditions in their own homes.

Chapter 12

Medication

I n earlier eras of psychiatry, there were only a few medications that could be prescribed for anxiety. The discovery of chlordiazepoxide in 1961 ushered in the era of the benzodiazepines or "minor tranquilizers" as they were then called. Several benzodiazepines were also available to be used as sleep aids. In 1966, K. L. Granville-Grossman and Paul Turner demonstrated the antianxiety effect of beta blockers on the physical symptoms of anxiety, such as tremors and palpitations, sometimes seen in public speakers.[1] At times, various medications which were then called "major tranquilizers," usually prescribed for psychosis, were used in small doses to calm anxiety. If the person was also depressed, we would use a tricyclic antidepressant, which has a sedating effect.

Today, there is a much wider range of medications that can be helpful if you are suffering from GAD, with overlapping conditions such as depression and other anxiety disorders or sleep problems. Using medications where appropriate for anxiety can be a tremendous aide to reducing emotional pain. Please remember that these are not "magic pills." You have to work with them to achieve success. Be patient. Some of them take a while to work.

You will fare better and be more likely to take your medication if you are an educated consumer. Understanding the pros and cons of various available treatments will allow you to be a better consumer and not just blindly sign up for a "cure." Medication education provides a basis for a collaborative effort between you and your physician to allow you to choose a plan with which you are most comfortable and which best meets your needs. For instance, in my office I might say to you, "There are three medications which I feel can be helpful to you." I would then explain the reasons for my choices, including advantages and possible side effects. You may have to choose between medications based on which side effects you are most willing to live with, such as weight gain, sexual side effects, sedation, etc. The knowledge gleaned from this chapter will help you communicate better with your physician and allow you to understand professional recommendations for medication management.

Benzodiazepines

This group of medications is the most widely prescribed in the world. Although they do give relief from anxiety, they should not be used indiscriminately. I only write a prescription for these medications if a client's anxiety symptoms are persistent, severe and impair daily functioning. There is some potential for abuse as well as physical and emotional dependency. The key to the choice of medication is client evaluation and management. This is done by taking a thorough history, educating the client and setting firm limits. I will avoid prescribing them if there is a history of alcohol or drug abuse or dependency. I find that anxious clients who are not prone to addiction are usually not a problem. Anxious clients in general are reluctant to take medications for any length of time. Many take a lower dose than prescribed. Although generally safe and effective, long-term use is discouraged.[2]

Maximum improvement usually is seen within the first four to six weeks of treatment. The most common side effects include drowsiness and unsteady movements. These medications are not for everyone. They can produce central nervous system side effects that mimic clinical depression. Although it is difficult to overdose lethally, they can produce additive central nervous system depression when taken with alcohol, other psychotropic medications, anticonvulsants, antihistamines or other depressant drugs. The physician can help avoid such problems by limiting his prescriptions to month-by-month and frequently reviewing the client's status by phone or in person. [3]

Care should be taken when stopping these products. Relapse, rebound anxiety or a true withdrawal syndrome is possible. Anxiety symptoms can return weeks or months later. Withdrawal symptoms, on the other hand, occur within two to ten days after the medication is stopped or lowered. They can include insomnia, dizziness, headaches, anorexia, vertigo, ringing in the ears, blurred vision and shakiness. These symptoms are different from those originally treated. They occur as blood levels decline and signal physical dependency. Physiological adaptation associated with long-term use causes these problems. Benzodiazepines selectively enhance GABA binding. In time, the body compensates for the presence of the antianxiety medication by lowering or ceasing production of the natural hormone GABA.

Therefore, do not stop these medications abruptly. If the benzodiazepines are tapered gradually, the body will resume its normal production of GABA and withdrawal symptoms will be minimized. In rebound anxiety, symptoms recur to greater than pretreatment levels. Unlike the new symptoms seen in withdrawal, rebound symptoms represent a worsening of the original symptoms and will gradually return to normal levels.

Do not drive, use machinery or do anything that requires mental alertness until you know how these medicines affect you. Do not stand or sit up quickly, especially if you are an older person. This reduces the risk of dizzy or fainting spells.[4]

Buspirone

This non-benzodiazepine antianxiety medication can be effective in clients with GAD who exhibit physical as well as emotional components of anxiety. It may take several weeks for buspirone to show effectiveness. Although tolerance and withdrawal symptoms are not an issue, symptoms rapidly return upon discontinuation. Its side effect profile shows minimal sedation, abuse potential or adverse interaction with alcohol or other central nervous system depressants. It is therefore often my agent of choice in treating anxiety in the former alcoholic, drug abuser or dependency-prone client. Side effects include dizziness, nausea, headaches, nervousness and lightheadedness. These can be minimized by starting at a low dose and gradually increasing the dose over a seven- to ten-day period. Some people experience a "woozy feeling" in their head when they first take it. This can be eliminated or diminished if the medication is taken with food.[5]

Meprobamate

This drug was very popular in the 1950s. Its side effect profile and tendency for withdrawal symptoms resembles those of barbiturates and it has a high abuse potential. Caroline Cassels, News Editor of Medscape Psychiatry Report, Medscape News wrote that the European Medicines Agency is recommending suspension throughout the European Union of all medications containing meprobamate.[6] I have included it only for historical reference. With the number of other antianxiety medications now available, it is infrequently prescribed.[7]

Antihistamines

This class can calm anxiety due to its sedative effects. Withdrawal reactions are not a problem. It can depress the seizure threshold and should be used with caution in people with a history of seizure disorder. It does not cause physical dependency or abuse and may therefore also be used as an alternative for people with addiction potential. I also offer it at times on an as-needed basis if someone is on an antianxiety agent and their anxiety is escalating. It is used in the emergency room intramuscularly to decrease acute anxiety. It can be used as a sleep aid on a short-term basis.[8]

Antidepressants

These medications, particularly the more sedative ones, are useful in treating GAD. They are particularly helpful in people with overlapping depression or sleep disturbances. They do require adequate dosage and several weeks to be effective for depression and anxiety. It is often difficult for the anxious person to wait so long for relief once they have sought treatment. The older group of antidepressants, the tricyclic antidepressants, discovered in the 1950s, tend to be sedative and can be helpful. The cyclic antidepressants block the absorption (reuptake) of the hormones (neurotransmitters) serotonin and norepinephrine, making more of these chemicals available in the brain. Their side effects include drowsiness, dry mouth, blurred vision, urinary retention, dizziness, decreased libido in women, delayed orgasm (retarded ejaculation) and low sex drive in men, weight gain and fatigue.[9]

The newer group of antidepressants, available since the 1990s, the selective serotonin reuptake inhibitors (SSRIs), is also helpful. I tend to prefer the more sedative ones. Some are more stimulating and initially can cause a person to feel jittery. Only one SSRI is currently approved by the Food and Drug Administration (FDA) for anxiety. These medications affect the levels of two naturally occurring chemicals in the brain: serotonin and norepinephrine. The most common side effects are constipation, dizziness, dry mouth, insomnia, loss of appetite, nausea, nervousness, sexual side effects, sleepiness, sweating and weakness.[10]

Bupropion

This is an antidepressant of the aminoketone class. It is chemically unrelated to other known antidepressant agents. Bupropion is a relatively weak inhibitor of the neuronal uptake of norepinephrine and dopamine. It has a low incidence of weight gain and sexual side effects. It is a good alternative if you are not tolerant of these side effects that are possible with other antidepressants. It can, however, cause dry mouth, headache and insomnia.[11]

Beta Blockers

These products, well known as antihypertensive agents, also have an antianxiety effect. They have no effect on the emotional manifestations of anxiety, but are helpful for peripheral physical symptoms of anxiety, such as hand tremors and palpitations. They are therefore most helpful with performance anxiety and are often taken by public speakers. A beta blocker is contraindicated in people with asthma, because it increases airway resistance, and in diabetes, because it affects carbohydrate and fat metabolism. It can lead to heart failure or conduction delays in people with a history of cardiac disease. Those who are being treated for angina or hypertension can experience an increase of symptoms when it is suddenly withdrawn.[12]

Antipsychotic Medications

The older group of antipsychotic medications, the major tranquilizers or neuroleptics, are used at times in small doses to control anxiety. They can be prescribed particularly when other antianxiety agents have failed or benzodiazepine abuse or dependency is an issue. The lowest effective dose should be used and the person must be monitored. Extrapyramidal (part of the motor nerve system) side effects are possible. They include tardive dyskinesia manifested by unwanted movements of the lips, face, hands, arms and feet, drug-induced Parkinsonism (sometimes called pseudo-Parkinsonism) which includes stiffness, shuffling gait, masked face or difficulties in rising from a sitting position, and dystonic reactions involving spasms of neck, back and other skeletal musculature. Another possible motor side effect is akathisia (an inner sense of restlessness or an uncontrollable drive to move the extremities). These side effects are treated with anticholinergic agents such as benzotropine or diphenhydrazine.[13]

The newer group of antipsychotic medications, called the atypical antipsychotics or second generation antipsychotics, can also be helpful in low doses for insomnia, anger management and anxiety. These are considered "off-label" uses (prscribed by physicians for an indication not approved by pharmaceutical companies) of these medications, which in higher doses are useful for bipolar disorder and schizophrenia. Side effects include weight gain, sluggishness, back pain, constipation, dry mouth, nausea and stuffy nose. They can precipitate diabetic symptoms in prone individuals.[14]

Insomnia Treatment

Many people with GAD have difficulty with their sleep patterns, either falling asleep, staying asleep or both. For the most part, the benzodiazepines and nonbenzodiazepines are short acting and last about four hours. In recent years, the nonbenzodiazepines are prescribed most often for insomnia. Both groups have possible side effects including fatigue, dizziness and difficulty with balance, and they can cause dependency and tolerance with long-term use. To prevent this problem, I tell clients to take their sleep medication for several days, get a good night's sleep and then not take it again until they don't sleep well for a night. Take sleep medication just before going to bed. Do not walk around or stay active for a prolonged time after taking it, because you will prevent it from working. Sleep aids should not be given to people with a history of drug or alcohol abuse or dependency.

Many anxious people have difficulty falling sleep because they are thinking, thinking and thinking. Cognitive-behavioral therapy (CBT), particularly relaxation therapy, can be helpful with this problem but will take a while.

Complementary Medicine

Herbal medicine has been undergoing a renaissance in the United States during recent years as the public seeks a low-cost, safe alternative to the more conventional antianxiety medications to treat their nervousness, tension, stress and sleep problems without the potential for physical addiction. There is only anecdotal knowledge that says that these supplements are helpful. All claims in reference to the products noted here are to be considered anecdotal in nature. More formal research is needed to clarify their therapeutic effectiveness and safety, compare them to standard medications and allow supplement standardization in reference to different extracts and doses. Although a prescription is not necessary to buy these products, I would encourage you to talk to your physician before taking them.

Kava Kava (Piper methysticum) is a green leafy member of the pepper family. Its name means "intoxicating pepper" in Latin. It is well known to the natives of the South Pacific islands for its tranquilizing properties and its ability to increase sociability. For centuries, its relaxing influence on the mind and body has been used at weddings and other special occasions such as welcoming ceremonies for dignitaries. It can also promote sleep. It is non-addictive and people rarely develop tolerance. It does not alter mental clarity or interfere with reaction time or alertness. Benefits can be noticed as early as the first or second week.[15]

The side effects of this botanical product include dermatitis, shortness of breath and visual disturbances (sensitivity to light and hallucinations). Excessive use for even three months can cause temporary yellowing of the skin, hair and nails. In rare cases, an allergic skin reaction can occur that involves a dry, scaly rash (first on the face and then on the rest of the body). Overindulging can lead to intoxication, disorientation, a loss of voluntary muscle control and a strong urge to sleep. Since it acts as a sedative, it should not be taken when driving or operating machinery. It should not be used with alcohol, barbiturates, antidepressants, tranquilizers or other substances that act on the central nervous system. Do not use if you are pregnant or breastfeeding, if you have Parkinson's or liver disease.[16]

Passion flower (Passiflora incarnate) is a mild herb which is native to the southeastern United States. In spite of its name, it is neither a stimulant nor an aphrodisiac. It is also known as Maypop. This botanical supplement is helpful for anxiety and can be used as a sedative/hypnotic. It does not produce tolerance, depression or sedation. Do not use if you are pregnant or nursing because it has not been tested in these situations.[17]

Valerian (Valeriana officinalis) is an herbal sedative obtained from a plant which is native to Europe and Asia. It can act as a minor tranquilizer for restlessness, anxiety and sleep disturbance. It also acts as a muscle relax-ant. The word comes from the Latin word for "well-being" and has been called "God's Valium." No significant side effects have been reported. When used for insomnia, it does not produce a morning hangover. It doesn't seem to interact with alcohol. However, it is a depressant and should not be used long term. Do not take if pregnant or nursing. Valerian has a distinctive odor (dirty socks) that is apparent when you open the product. This odor will not affect your breath. It is sold as a tea, tincture or extract.[18]

Chamomile (Matricaria recutita), called the gentle herb, is a flowering plant in the daisy family that is native to Europe and Asia. This herb has mildly sedating and muscle-relaxing effects. It is used to treat stress and insomnia. It comes in capsule, liquid and tea form. Chamomile contains coumarin, a naturally-occurring blood thinner. It should not be combined with other medications or supplements that have the same effect. It should not be used by people who have a bleeding disorder or two weeks before or after surgery. Do not take during pregnancy or breastfeeding.[19]

In the United States, all drugs must be approved as safe and effective by the FDA. This is a costly and time-consuming process that can take up to eight to ten years from initial filing of the investigational new drug application through three phases of clinical trials to approval for physician prescription. Newly approved products are then typically granted exclusivity for five years, which necessitates a huge marketing initiative by the pharmaceutical companies to make up their expenditures and make a profit in the narrow window of opportunity before a generic equivalent appears in the marketplace.

Plants are not patentable. Herbal medicines, unlike pharmacological drugs, are often composed of several components which work together to produce a combined effect. Approval by the FDA would require that every active compound in a single plant extract be evaluated for safety and efficacy. These economic and legal issues combine to deter pharmaceutical companies from taking the initiative to produce such natural products.

Many people are reluctant to seek therapy due to fears of what they will learn about themselves. Many are unwilling to use antianxiety medications due to concerns of dependency, withdrawal and loss of control. Many feel ashamed or embarrassed to seek help or would rather do it themselves. I hope that these last two chapters, in educating you about the multiple treatment possibilities available for anxiety, will help you face these demons and feel more secure in seeking treatment for this common disorder. If you have been anxious all your life, help is available. Talk your options over with your physician and counselor to see which are best suited for you and your particular mental health situation.

Part III

High Stress Situations

Chapter 13

Anxiety and Adult Attention Deficit Disorder

The adult client who presents with a childhood history of Attention Deficit Hyperactivity Disorder (ADHD) or Attention Deficit Disorder (ADD) and current anxiety presents a particular diagnostic problem. A good history is the key to untangling the situation. GAD is an inherited biological illness. Clients with GAD will usually report that they have been nervous all of their lives, have an anxious relative or two and have the four cardinal complaints that we discussed earlier. They have physical and mental symptoms that we noted before. These clients may have other psychiatric problems or may overlap with some of the emotional and physical symptoms that we mentioned previously. To make things even more confusing, the anxious person may not always have GAD at all. A degree of anxiety may be normal, and even helpful, before a test or a presentation at work. Anxiety can also be a normal reaction to stress.

ADHD/ADD persists into adulthood in 70 percent of those who have symptoms in childhood. Epidemiological studies in the United States have placed its prevalence at 4.4 percent in adults.[1] ADHD/ADD does not always show a family history. Genetics can play a role, however. Other risk factors include mothers who drink alcohol and/or smoke during pregnancy, low birth weight and fetal brain injuries. Separating these two disorders is further complicated because GAD can mimic the symptoms of ADHD. Anxiety may cause restlessness that one can interpret as hyperactivity. Persistent worries or

151

concerns may cause a person to be inattentive. As anxiety increases, people may act quickly or irrationally in order to minimize stress. Girls in childhood often present with attention problems and over-talkativeness rather than hyperactivity. Boys and girls may have ADD with secondary anxiety due to the frustrations, failures and negative feedback that they have experienced all of their lives. Each of these factors can cause diagnostic confusion that can follow through to adulthood.

People with ADHD or ADD usually have a history of learning or behavioral problems in school. They often have to work harder than other children to achieve the same scholastic results. Often they are bright, but do not do well in school due to the classic symptoms of:

- Hyperactivity
- Inattention/Easy Distractibility
- Impulsivity

Children with ADHD may lack behavioral inhibition. They may have flares of temper that keep them from participating in sporting events or bring on the wrath of negative or critical coaches. Continued education about the ramifications of this disorder is important to allow adults to put the child's responses in perspective. Some students may find that they learn better if they hear the instructions or information. Others learn better if they read the material directly. These are different pathways through which information can enter the brain and may help increase comprehension at school or at work.

Only a percentage of children with ADHD continue to meet the criteria for ADHD as they age. Most hyperactive/impulsive symptoms decline as people with ADHD approach adulthood. Inattention tends to persist into adulthood. Adult ADHD clients complain of difficulty with concentration and short-term memory. Anxiety and low self-esteem are often the most common residual symptoms of childhood ADHD or ADD. Adult clients with these disorders are often chronically frustrated. On some level they know that they are smart, but have spent most of their life failing, not living up to their potential and feeling stupid. ADHD may present in adulthood as disorganization, difficulty finishing tasks, job instability or marital problems.

People may not always show their symptoms. Some adults have developed the discipline to dampen the hyperactive/impulsive symptoms in certain situations. Most have developed coping mechanisms to compensate for their impairment. Passion trumps anxiety; thus, if people feel passionate about something, they may be able to overcome their anxiety and/or their ADHD/ADD symptoms and complete the task.

A hasty diagnosis can suggest that the person has ADHD/ADD when he or she really has an anxiety disorder or perhaps both. The treatments differ for GAD compared to ADHD/ADD. We've already covered those of GAD thoroughly. Treatment for adult ADD can include individual psychotherapy to deal with education, reassurance and issues of low self-esteem. The therapist-client relationship can be a corrective emotional experience if interpersonal problems are an issue. Cognitive-behavioral therapy (CBT) may help some adults with ADHD/ADD improve functionality. However, the main thrust of treatment for adult ADHD/ADD is pharmacotherapy. Doses may vary and must be titrated for the individual client and his or her unique situation. Numerous stimulants are available that can often show results within the first week.

Unfortunately, these products have an addiction and abuse potential. They should not be used by people with a history of or an active problem with alcohol or drug dependency or abuse, or if there is a family history of addiction. These medications may have a risk of cardiovascular side effects. It is important to obtain medical clearance for people who have problems in this area. There are also other medications including non-stimulants and antidepressants that can be helpful and are not addicting. Discuss the possibilities and the pros and cons with your physician so that you can better choose the medication that is appropriate for you.

If primary anxiety is the issue, an antianxiety agent may be the treatment of choice. If adult ADHD or ADD with secondary anxiety is the problem, treat the ADD and the anxiety usually abates. If both ADHD and GAD are present, you may need to use two different medications or approaches. If some other medical or psychiatric disorder is causing the anxiety, treat the other disorder first. If you identify with the symptom clusters above, ask your physician to evaluate you. Help is available for you; all of these disorders are treatable. Let us see how it played out in Chelsey's life.

Chelsey's Story

"My anxiety is my biggest life challenge. It challenges me in many ways that may go unnoticed by those around me, but I myself can feel and see what my anxiety can and has done to me in my life. The first time I experienced anxiety, my heart felt like it was literally going to come out of my body. I was short of breath. It was then that I knew something was not right. I didn't think there was something "wrong" with me particularly, but I knew that the racing heart, constant worry and fear of not being able to control it truly scared me.

"I feel as if I always used an inner defense mechanism where I would push all my feelings aside, I would ignore them to the point where I felt completely numb. Doing this only made my anxiety a million times worse. At first I truly didn't want to believe it, I didn't want to have my heart racing so fast that I felt like I couldn't breathe and the biggest question I kept asking myself was 'WHY IS THIS HAPPENING TO ME?' I would then panic and think that something was obviously wrong with me mentally or physically, which again only made it worse.

"I would start to think, 'I'm losing my mind.' My anxiety got to the point where I knew deep in my heart that I needed to do something to alleviate it and get to the core of what triggers it or find out if there was something else going on along with my anxiety. It was time for me to put my pride aside and see a doctor."

Chelsey looked younger than her twenty-five years. Her complaints in our first session involved anxiety and issues with her mother, who had developed Parkinsonism five years previously and recently had undergone knee replacement surgery. Chelsey had no personal history of drug or alcohol abuse or dependency. She had no significant medical problems and no allergies. She mentioned that at eighteen, she had gone to a religious retreat for teenagers. They had her write a letter about her personal problems and then read it out loud to the group. Their feedback helped her, because it allowed her to realize that she was not alone. She felt that it was time to come to therapy and try to express herself again.

Chelsey was raised in a working class neighborhood in a suburb of Philadelphia. She lived with her family in the same small, three-bedroom row house in which she had been born. Her mother was an anxious woman who worried excessively. She had worked as a waitress, leaving little Chelsey to be taken care of by her fourteen-year-older sister. When this sister got married and left, Chelsey was eleven. Chelsey was then alone and forced to grow up quickly behaviorally, which explained her tendency to maintain a façade of being independent. She shared a bed and a room with her younger sister. A brother, fifteen years older, was also out of the house. Her father, a plumber, suffered from post-traumatic stress disorder from the Vietnam War and was a recovering alcoholic, dry for twenty-four years, who still attended Alcoholics Anonymous meetings. He was nervous and a worrier. She told me that he was "a good man," but had little tolerance, was impatient, had a bad temper and could "spaz out." "I have the same temperament," Chelsey shared. "He often yelled at my mother and sister, but not at me."

The small house was in constant chaos and did not offer much privacy. When she was a youngster, there were thirteen people living in the house including her sister, brother-in-law, aunt and niece. In a family revolving around an alcoholic (even one sober for twenty-four years), we often talk about people having "roles." Chelsey's role was to be the "little soldier," who kept the peace, acted as the "middleman" and took care of everyone's needs. This part fit her well, in that she was a people pleaser who wanted to be liked and who worried about what other people thought of her. She said that her main stressor was "people." Her mother's anxiety and constant demands came in waves, trying to knock her over. When she arrived for therapy, she had reached the boiling point and was very conflicted and angry at her mother. "It's sad that Mom is sick," Chelsey said. "I feel guilty that I am angry. I'm concerned, but I don't want to be an enabler. If she really cannot do something, I would be glad to help. But if she can do it herself, I want her to do it herself."

Chelsey initially reported the classic GAD triad of anxiety, worry and avoidance. She experienced physical symptoms like shortness of breath and palpitations. However, as I got to know Chelsey better, it seemed that there were other issues. She had gone to private school. She did well there but had to work hard because, as she admitted, she was easily distracted. She had difficulty understanding why she had to work harder than others when people told her she was bright. Often, she though that she was a crazy person. I asked her to fill out an Adult Self-Report Scale (ASRS) Symptom Checklist for ADHD or ADD. This is just a screener, but can often lead us in an accurate diagnostic direction, particularly if the results line up with the client's childhood history. She finished with high scores in attention problems, weak organizational skills, procrastination, being easily distracted, fidgeting, restlessness, difficulty relaxing, intrusiveness and impatience. Her score meant that it was "highly likely" that she had ADD.

Chelsey's Opinion of What Helped Her Anxiety

"After my first session with Dr. Zal was the first time in a very long time that I actually felt hope and faith that I was going to be okay. He communicated with me and instantly made me feel comfortable, which makes it a whole lot easier to open up! After several sessions, I started to realize that it was not just anxiety that was bothering me. I also felt easily irritated, impulsive and distracted at work. I couldn't sleep; I would range around three to four hours of sleep per night. I told Dr. Zal my symptoms and how it seemed very obvious that there was something else that was going on. He asked me more questions about my childhood, my performance in school and my problems at work. I knew that I was anxious but now I was also diagnosed with Attention Deficit Disorder (ADD). What a relief to finally know what was wrong.

"When I looked back to my younger years it all started to come together for me. I remember not paying attention, being easily distracted and walking into things such as people, walls and so forth. I remember my father always saying to me, 'Chelsey, you need to pay attention!' in a stern voice. I would just look at him and think to myself 'I didn't even do anything!' It took me almost twenty-five years to realize that I had ADD. I am not sure why I was never tested for it in the past. It is something that my sister has and also my younger nephew. After I was diagnosed, I was placed on medication for it. I can't even begin to explain how much happier I am, how I finally feel that my life is actually coming together. Most important, I don't feel vulnerable to my own self. I now know that there is nothing wrong with me, which was what I used to convince myself of all the time. I am more focused, not easily irritated, not angered over little things anymore and also my anxiety has been reduced significantly.

"Now I know that I cannot just 'get rid' of anxiety, but there are plenty of ways to ease it. Talking to Dr. Zal is one way of easing my anxiety. Exercise also helps. I go to the gym or work out at home. I have taught fitness classes and hope to do it again. I felt hopeless until I found this psychiatrist and started seeing him regularly. I have learned how to deal with my anxiety better. Knowing that I not only have anxiety but also ADD enables me to understand how the two can co-relate. Furthermore, Dr. Zal has helped me realize things about myself that I was blind to. I always thought I was the problem. With his help and expertise, I can finally say that I am not the problem. I have come a long way since the first time I came to his office.

"Anxiety and ADD can be scary. Some patients don't want to believe these can be their problems. Most people internalize and try to bury their own self-issues, but that will not work. Expressing, understanding and listening to yourself and seeking help will benefit you more in the long run than anything else. Talking to a therapist has helped me in my own life. I believe it's good to discuss your anxiety and other issues that you may have with someone who is impartial. While we can all talk to our friends about problems we are having, the people that care the most and can help you are, in my opinion, your family and your doctors. These are the people you should rely on. Friends may come and go; family stays forever. When I first started therapy, I found a quote I truly live by and it has helped me very much with my own anxiety 'Avoid your fears and they begin to grow, move towards them and they dampen.'[2] The more you try to resolve the issues you may be dealing with in your life, the further you will go; the more you try to push them aside, the more they will grow."

My Opinion of What Helped Chelsey's Anxiety

Chelsey had been having trouble falling asleep, because she couldn't stop thinking and reviewing the day. I asked her to try a sleep medication for insomnia. She reported at our next session that "it has really helped" and that she had slept a full six hours. She refused to take any other medication, because she felt that her mother's antidepressant medication made her mother "crazy." At our third session, Chelsey revealed that she had had one panic attack four years earlier. She continued to complain of anxiety symptoms, including feeling hot, shortness of breath, palpitations and nausea. We talked it over and she allowed me to add a medication for her anxiety. She subsequently reported that she was doing better on this medication. She said that her anxiety came down from a ten to a four. Her mood also improved.

Later in our sessions, she revealed that she was having problems at work, because she was easily distracted and could not focus. She told me that her sister had ADD and that she herself had been easily distracted in elementary school. She had not been hyperactive, which is not unusual. Boys are more likely to be hyperactive in childhood and be diagnosed with ADHD than girls. I started her on an antidepressant for her ADD. Two weeks later, she felt that, "It made a difference. I'm concentrating better. I'm not forgetful. I'm more organized."

Initially, Chelsey joked that "people" were her problem. She mentioned her mother and friends, both men and women. Since childhood, her relationship with her mother was conflicted and difficult. Her mother did not screen her thoughts and said exactly what she felt, which was often negative. "It really gets on my nerves," Chelsey said. She also resented that her mother had worked and had not been available to her as a child. She resented having to play her role in an alcoholic family dynamic. More recently, she resented having to help her mother so much. Initially, I stressed that she try to accept her mother as she was at the time and not continue to see her as she was ten to fifteen years ago. At age sixty-three and now retired, her mother was dealing with a chronic illness and was not the same woman she had been during Chelsey's childhood. Chelsey admitted that she felt loved by her mother. As with many clients, Chelsey came to realize that her mother had her own troubles and did the best that she could. She realized that her mother had worked because they needed the money, not because she wanted to avoid her daughter. As she felt stronger, she began to set time limits on her mother. They started to get along better.

Men were also a problem for Chelsey. This was not surprising considering her emotionally volatile and abusive father, her isolation as a child and her need to please others to obtain love and attention. She tended to choose boyfriends based on what we call in therapy "the repetition compulsion." We choose people who resemble people in the past with whom we have unresolved issues. Our mind says, "This time it will be different. It will work out better. I will get what I really want." Usually it does not work. Chelsey's first serious boyfriend at age seventeen followed this pattern. Initially, things went well. He was affectionate and involved. They saw each other several times a week. After three years of dating, they moved in together. In time, however, he started to hit her. She felt powerless: "He made me think that it was my fault. I felt that I was so in love with him. I felt that he was the one." She finally had him arrested for domestic violence and was able to move on. After this "bad relationship," she went for outpatient therapy for one year.

Girlfriends were also a problem for Chelsey. She was friendly with some young women that she knew in high school. Emotionally, they never left high school—petty jealousy and meanness were the norm. Chelsey tried to play the role that she knew from childhood. However, being the supportive middleman here did not bring positive results. These young women rarely met her expectations. Chelsey tried to please them by being helpful and taking their bad advice and suggestions. If they were displeased, they would make her feel guilty or ignore her. She was constantly upset and frustrated over her friendships and her expectations. In therapy, we worked on having her use her own judgment, making decisions that were good for her and based on what she wanted and taking responsibility for her actions. As her self-esteem improved in treatment, she was better able to do this and take the risk that they might not approve.

I told her that she needed to focus on her own quality of life and not just spend her energies on finding a mate. It is nice to have a significant other but he should add to your life and not be your entire world. There were one or two false starts but she eventually began dating a young man whom she met at a wedding. He was very different from her past relationships and was not part of her high school group. She made other positive changes. She had been working at the same firm since she was fifteen. She always worried that people would not like her if she advanced. However, when she was laid off recently, she quickly found another job with better benefits and more responsibility. She even talked about going back to college to obtain a master's degree.

Individual psychotherapy, in combination with an antianxiety medication and a long-acting amphetamine, was helpful in calming her down and giving her a new perspective on her situation. It improved her mood and self-esteem and allowed her to feel more in control when dealing with people. She was happy to learn that she was not going crazy. I hope Chelsey continues to break out of her childhood socio-economic and emotional restraints and continues to develop her true potential in the larger world outside her little dwelling in the neighborhood of her youth.

Chapter 14

Anxiety and Chronic Illness

A chronic physical illness can be a difficult challenge to negotiate for anyone. For the individual with GAD, it is complicated by anxiety, worry, negativity, avoidance, moodiness and depression. Life can change in a flash—one minute you feel that you are healthy and okay but the next instant you are diagnosed with a chronic physical illness. There may even be a feeling of some relief when you know what is wrong, because perhaps something has not felt right for a while. The overwhelming first emotion is fear. You are frightened of where all this will lead. There is fear of the unknown. Will I suffer? Will I ever be the same? Will I die? Lost in your own thoughts, you are probably not even hearing half of what the doctor is saying. You have a lot to learn about your disease and about what the future holds. Lack of information only grows our fears.

In the middle of all of these questions, your mind is filled with overwhelming feelings of sadness and loss. Has the person I have felt I am disappeared? Will I ever be my old self again? Will I be able to do all of the old things that I loved? Will I be able to travel, play sports, have sex, take care of myself and support myself and my family? Are all my goals and dreams still attainable or have they been lost forever? Many dark thoughts course through your mind. Will my close friends and family abandon me? Will I be a burden to my spouse? Will anyone still love me? Will I be a failure? Most clients who have chronic illnesses will eventually find that the quality of their lives will be different, but not necessarily terrible. Hopefully, you will have the courage to look closely at your doubts and fears and refuse to be intimidated by this negative mindset.

Remember, your chronic illness also affects every member of your family. It may be hard for many of them to cope with this major change in their lives or the expectations that they had for you. Initially, this may lead to increased anger and irritability. It can also result in their showing you additional attention, love and affection. Like many other major life changes, it can draw you closer together or push you farther apart. Take the time to adjust to the new situation and give your loved ones time to adjust. You may all go through different phases. The end result depends on the attitude that is chosen by all. As with other times of important communication, try to share how you feel and not blame the other person. Be empathetic and let your love shine through.

Your medical situation will also affect your friends and your work colleagues. Some may ignore or even distance themselves from the entire situation, because they do not know what to say or do. Some may show surprise, concern, empathy and support. After a while, you may get tired of hearing "How are you feeling?" and would rather hear "Good to see you." Later on, some of those around you may start to tell you to stop complaining and just adjust, which is not easy. Let's see if Stan can discover control, a new acceptance and contentment.

Stan's Story

"My anxiety is my life. I worry about everything. I would feel uncomfortable as a child, but didn't know what it was. They said that my aunt was 'high strung.' I never heard of an anxiety attack growing up. Later on I realized that my mother's father, who was angry all the time, had anxiety attacks. As an adult, I get nervous several times a month. These attacks are usually related to something specific that I'm fixated on or worried about. I get anxious, tense and irritable. I feel cold, queasy in my stomach and sometimes lightheaded. My palms

*sweat. My lower back can ache. I have muscle tension. I have diffi-
culty sleeping.*

"*Years ago, my current and third wife, Lana, was diagnosed
with stage three ovarian cancer. I remember sitting in the doctor's
office when he told us. I don't remember anything after that. I got hot,
dizzy and almost fell out of the chair. I read everything I could about
the cancer. All I could think about was my wife's funeral. This visit
was followed by surgery, chemotherapy, CT scans and constant visits
to doctors. After this, I was bummed out and my anxiety got worse. It
upset me to see her sick. I didn't want to see her hurt. She is doing well
now; she beat the odds and is fine. However, I still worry and think
that I am going to lose her. She's my best friend. I love her. I need her.
She handles everything.*

"*Sometimes, I can have a really 'bad anxiety attack' and have a
'meltdown.' At these times, I get so dizzy, vomit and can't even stand
up. I lie on the bathroom floor. Afterwards, I feel totally wiped out
and at times don't feel right until the next day. I was a commercial
pilot for a private company and therefore could not take any medicine. Occasionally, I would feel anxious on a flight, when things were
not going perfectly. I would lie and say it must have been something
that I ate. Sometimes, I would beg off flying and suffer as a co-pilot
with just radio duties.*

"*When I first met Dr. Zal, I told him that I was in excellent
health. Sometime later, I started having visual issues, where I could
not focus in one eye. I went to an ophthalmologist. He said that my
eyes were healthy but that he could not correct my vision to twen-
ty-twenty. I felt something was wrong. I went back. He said 'this can
open up a whole can of worms' and referred me to a neurologist. The
neurologist ordered a lumbar puncture, an MRI of the brain and an
evoked potential test of my eyesight. All three came back abnormal.
The doctor suspected multiple sclerosis. He wanted me to start on
medication but I told him that I wasn't ready for that yet. I got a*

second opinion. The second doctor wasn't definitive and told me to get another MRI in six months. Soon, I started having the same problem with my other eye. I went on short-term disability. After six months, I realized that I could not fly and I retired.

"Things stayed the same for a while. Then I caught the flu. Soon thereafter, I started having other neurological symptoms. I developed neuropathy in my feet and weakness of my legs, which progressed to stiffness. I was told that a viral infection can aggravate neurological symptoms. I then developed problems with my balance. All of this has made my anxiety worse, because I do not know how bad this is going to get and no one can tell me what the future holds."

Although he did not say it directly, Stan was very worried and afraid of the illness that seemed to be taking over his body. As he admitted, Stan had been anxious all of his life although he did not always know what he was experiencing. He came for treatment initially because his wife pressured him. He only said, "I have not been comfortable." During our first session, I did a lengthy psychiatric evaluation, including a medical history, psychosocial history and mental status evaluation. His psychiatric history revealed that he had had counseling at age fifteen for "school problems" and had a relative who was "high strung." He showed no significant medical problems and no history of drug or alcohol abuse or dependency. Toward the end of the session, he admitted that his wife's illness got him thinking about mortality and what could happen to him in the future: "Now everything seems like a big deal. Sometimes I feel like the pavement will give way." I believed that he was suffering from GAD and an adjustment disorder with depressed mood that coincided with his wife's cancer diagnosis. I asked him to make a commitment to individual psychotherapy. He agreed to come and talk.

At our second session, I asked him to describe his parents. This often will give me clues as to how the client sees other people in his or her life. He described his mother as a perfectionist who could be controlling, demanding and opinionated. "My mother was very attractive," he said. "She was beautiful, with blond hair and blue eyes. She was affectionate but could yell and scream and used a belt for discipline. She was the man in charge." He told me that his father, an engineer, was honest and responsible although not driven in business: "He didn't like confrontation. He had a tremendously high boiling point. When my mother fought with him, he would never fight back. He graduated college even though he was a poor student. He was affectionate but he never did anything with me. He was totally oblivious and passive. He didn't take charge of anything. He didn't give me any direction. I wish that he had been more of a father." I noticed as our sessions continued that being assertive and proactive were not Stan's strong qualities either.

At another session, I asked him about his high school experience, his "school problems" and why he decided to get counseling. He explained, "My mother had expectations for what I was going to be. If I got a B grade on a test, she would say, 'You're not average. You are better than that. I will accept nothing but As.' She always backed you into a corner and you couldn't get away. I was afraid to speak up. My sister was bright and thought to have high potential. I, on the other hand, came across anxious and depressed. Feelings like these were also not acceptable. I believed that everybody thought I was stupid and would end up in a dead-end job. I felt 'What's the use. I can't win.' At age sixteen, I cursed at my mother. I quit high school four months before graduation, because I knew that it would stick it to my mother. I was angry about everything. Nothing was ever good enough for her." Stan saw his mother as strong. It was a double-edged sword. He wanted to separate from her, but was afraid that he would fail and wouldn't be all right without her. Part of him felt that he still needed her as a safety net. This was a major part of his rebellion and his adolescent struggle.

Stan eventually obtained his high school general equivalency diploma (GED). A few months later, looking for unconditional love and barely twenty years old, he became attracted to Cathy, a beautiful girl whom he had known for a while. They soon got engaged and he moved with her to a college campus in Pennsylvania so she could attend school. Stan immediately went to the dean and asked to enter school. He was told that if he did well in his classes for one semester that the dean would allow him to matriculate at the college. He did well and entered school. Stan and Cathy came home for the holidays and got married. He soon told his new wife that he had dreamed of taking the civil service state police exam since he'd been seventeen. He said that he would take the exam and if he passed, he would work as a state policeman and continue school closer to home. Cathy was not happy about his desire to be a state policeman. Four months later, his mother-in-law came to visit and convinced his wife to return home, because she didn't feel that Stan was good enough for her daughter. They divorced. Hurt, devastated and once again feeling defeated, Stan quit school and also returned home. He found an apartment and got a job with a contractor building home additions.

Eventually, Stan got a job with the state police and was happy. Five years later, he fell in love and married Beth, a "gorgeous" woman who "looked like a movie star." Beth, however, was not happy. She told him, "I got married too young. I haven't lived my life. I never partied or had fun." At his insistence, Beth and Stan went for marital therapy. Yet she remained discontented. Her parents liked Stan, told their daughter that they felt that he was a good guy and encouraged her to stay put. Nevertheless, after a little over a year of marriage, they separated and later divorced. Stan remained single for eleven years. During this time he pursued another dream. As a hobby, he had obtained a private pilot's license. His roommate at the time was a pilot who was able to act as his flying instructor. Subsequently, Stan obtained a commercial and instructor's rating to fly. Eventually, he retired from the state police and got a job as a co-pilot flying private planes for a large corporation.

After years of bachelorhood, he went out for dinner one night with friends and met Lana. He described her as "the most off-the-wall woman I had ever met. She was like a left-wing communist. I was pretty conservative at the time." He continued to see her and found her to be "smart, feisty and sexy. There was something about her. We had intelligent conversations. We talked about stuff. She was the first person with whom I had ever had a serious conversation. We found that we both had been going out with a lot of people and were unfulfilled. We hit it off. We found that we were a lot alike." They continued to date and were married the following year. Lana took over the family business when her father died and still ran it on a daily basis. Stan and Lana had a long and significant history together. They went through a lot as a couple, including parental death, illness and family problems. They had much in common: friends, a common background and similar values. They shared an interest in vacations with friends, gadgets and a love for dogs. Both in their late thirties when they married, they discussed parenthood very little and ended up not having children. In spite of their frequent arguments, they were very supportive of one another and were always there for each other. They had two dogs they loved and to whom they were devoted.

Stan's Opinion of What Helped His Anxiety

"My wife, Lana, also suffers from anxiety. She used to have panic attacks. We were in a local book store one day and happened to see a book on the topic of panic and anxiety attacks. I picked it up and looked at the dust jacket. Much to my surprise, the author was a local doctor. That started her and ultimately my association with Dr. Zal.

"When I first went for treatment, I couldn't take medication, because I was a pilot. I now take a daily antidepressant and antianxiety medication. They have helped. They have minimized the anxiety attacks, although occasionally anxiety breaks through. My mood is not as bad now. It is more even than it was before. It helps to talk out my frustrations. I used to beat myself up and be over-concerned about what other people thought. I try not to do that as much anymore. I try to follow through on what I really want. I am trying to be more active and less passive. I have learned that I look at everything as the worst case scenario. I am trying to accept myself as being human and less than perfect. I have to be more positive in my attitude and do what I can within my present capabilities—my new normal. I know that I do not have control over my medical condition. I am trying to control what I can in my life. My wife and I recently went on a flat-boat river cruise. Making the decision to go was hard. I worried a lot and was uptight about making the trip. I finally agreed to go. I met other people who have disabilities. We could not do everything on all the shore excursions. Sometimes we just sat and talked. However, we had a great time and I was thankful that we were there. Even with all its trials and tribulations, life is not as bad as it could be. It could be worse."

My Opinion of What Helped Stan's Anxiety

At the end of our initial session, I asked Stan what his goals were for therapy. After some thought, he mentioned that he wanted to sleep better, work on his sex life with his wife and feel more secure. I knew that this wasn't the whole story of what we would need to work on in treatment, but at least his suggestions were a way to start.

People with GAD often have problems falling and staying asleep, particularly when they are under additional stress. They can experience restless, unsatisfying sleep. Stan also admitted that he felt depressed "off and on" and was having "crazy, vivid dreams." A common theory is that the GAD client's dreams are still working on problems, conflicts and wishes. I taught Stan good sleep hygiene and suggested that he find some way to unwind and relax before getting into bed. This can include such things as a warm shower or bath, a glass of warm milk, doing a puzzle or anything else that can allow you to unwind. I told him, "Don't watch stimulating movies or television shows before bedtime. Only use your bed for sleeping or sex." If all else fails, there are sleeping medications available that can be taken on a short-term basis to break the cycle of sleeplessness.

In reference to his sex life, Stan was upset because he and his wife had not been intimate in some time. Several factors contributed to this. Obviously number one was Lana's cancer and her physical condition. I asked him to talk to his wife and tell her that he missed being physically close with her. I suggested that he ask her to talk to her physicians about what was practical. This roadblock brought back other, older problems. When he had first met her, Stan felt that Lana was "sexy." However, over time, he said that she was a good wife but really very uptight about sex. She also put a lot of energy into her work responsibilities. I recommended increasing affection and fore-play and trying to be physically close even if they did not have intercourse. I suggested that he initiate more and not just get frustrated waiting for her signals. I shared what I call the "rule of threes." If you both want to have sex, it's a go. If your partner wants to and you really do not, say no in a way that doesn't foster the appearance of rejection. If you are neutral try to be accom-modating. This is part of a long-term relationship. I told him that anger and tension can dampen desire. He promised to think about these issues and try to be more understanding and more active.

Lana also had GAD. This often impinged on their interaction, both sexually and otherwise. Their relationship was always contentious. Many of their fights were caused or escalated when they were both anxious at the same time. This is something that I tried to point out to them. When they were both feeling anxious, I suggested that it was a good idea to postpone the discussion before it escalated or they said things that they regretted. I recom-mended, "Take a break. Discuss it later after you both have calmed down." Stan often remarked, "My wife is cocksure about everything. It's hard for her to admit that she is wrong. I think that my mother wanted my father to fight back. He never did. I always fight back. I'm not a wimp!" This is not always the best response in a marital relationship. At a later date, I pointed this out to Stan. He realized that he was overcompensating for his father's passivity and perhaps had a distorted view of what made a man.

Security is also multifaceted. It involves your need for support as well as your self-esteem and how you see yourself and the world. At our initial session, when Stan first mentioned wanting to feel more secure, I made a mental note to ask him about his parents at a future time. In therapy, Stan learned that he grew up feeling inadequate starting in his childhood home. Later he compensated for these feelings by becoming a state police officer and a pilot, which allowed him to feel more in control of his world. Although very capable, he grew to feel that he needed outside support to survive. His wife's cancer brought these feelings forward again. His anxiety escalated as he realized on some level how much he needed her and how dependent he had become on her. Anxiety, feelings of inadequacy and anger at the females in his life at the time accounted for his not completing his education in high school and later in college. When he started having neurological problems he once again gravitated instinctively back to education. Using a large magnifying glass over the screen, he started taking computer courses to get his college degree. He started to realize that it was something that he really wanted to accomplish for himself and not because others demanded it. He did very well academically, which helped his self-esteem.

When Stan began having neurological symptoms, we had to shift gears a little in therapy. Our efforts focused more on helping him overcome feelings of depression, sorrow and helplessness. During times of increased symptoms, I saw him more and tried to be supportive while helping him focus on the positive. He suffered great losses, including his identity, his career, independence and physical ability. "My pilot's license came up for renewal," Stan said. "I turned it down. That was tough. It was like losing a leg. I was pretty depressed." We talked about focusing on what he can do, rather than what he cannot do, and I have emphasized his taking a problem-solving approach to his situation. He is a "master of avoidance." When he could no longer drive, he finally arranged with a local transportation company to bring him to the office.

We talked about ways that he can dissipate his frustration and worry. I encouraged him to continue to exercise up to his limits. I pushed him to reduce isolation and stay involved in the world and in touch with his friends. He had a friend on the west coast who also had multiple sclerosis; talking to him was helpful. I continued to prompt Stan to have realistic expectations, to take care of himself and to ask for help when needed. Fortunately, he had a caring wife and a group of supportive friends who continually pushed him to stay involved. His problem-solving skills improved. He researched things and gained a good amount of information about his illness and the available resources. He saw a counselor who dealt with the visually-impaired and involved himself in a low-vision program. Stan's biggest fear was of going blind. His anxiety and avoidance often stood in the way of his moving forward. However, he tried and that is the most important thing. Life can only improve if you try.

I saw Stan recently. I opened the waiting room door and there he was, a thin, balding man with salt and pepper hair, sitting in a chair at the other end of the square room looking forlorn, staring into space as the television droned and the other clients read magazines or talked. He was wearing jeans, a gray sweatshirt and sneakers. He has been growing a beard and mustache, which is coming in with a lot of gray. Because of his diminished vision, he did not know that I was there until I called his name. He immediately got up, trying to stand as straight and tall as he could, but having to lean on his cane for support. He slowly walked toward my voice and announced, "It is not a good day."

I followed behind him as he continued to walk down the hall toward my consultation room, weaving slightly to the right and holding on to the wall at times to keep his balance. It indeed was not a good day. I have seen him walk better. I felt sad and thought to myself, *What I wish for Stan is that he has many additional good days. He has more courage and fortitude than he realizes. I hope that his neurological illness progresses slowly. Using all of my psychiatric skills, I will try my best to keep him calm. I will continue to try to keep his mood elevated and his emotional ship on course and stabilized. I am hopeful that psychiatric treatment continues to be helpful to Stan as he deals with his life issues and his chronic illness.*

Chapter 15

Anxiety in the Elderly

GAD may be the most common mental disorder among the elderly. In this age group, anxiety is more common than even depression, particularly in females, but the diagnosis can be difficult to make in older people. They are more prone to vague bodily symptoms and they often complain of fatigue, insomnia, aches and pains and bowel symptoms. Sleep problems particularly can signify anxiety in the elderly and overlapping symptoms such as depression, dementia and substance abuse can mask and/or signify anxiety. Primary medical problems such as irritable bowel syndrome, asthma/COPD, diabetes and thyroid disease can manifest anxiety. Hyperthyroidism, hypertension and cardiac arrhythmias can also cause anxiety. Medications such as steroids, inhalers and theophylline can trigger anxiety-like symptoms.

Senior citizens, confronted with the emotional and physical demands and changes of old age, face new challenges in coping with life. The elderly are prone to real-life stressors such as illness, disability, widowhood, financial distress and social isolation. Alone and gradually losing their physical abilities and the people in their lives, they often can feel helpless, frightened and anxious. Anxiety in the elderly can cause them to avoid and withdraw and can affect the quality of their lives. Caregivers and health professionals often ignore anxiety in the elderly, feeling that it is just a normal part of aging. Acknowledging it can be helpful and therapeutic.

We will all grow older. Other cultures have different attitudes toward the aged. The Chinese revere their elders for their wisdom and experience. In India, people have a tremendous sense of duty and responsibility toward their older relatives. In these societies, elderly people are honored as symbols of humanity and divinity and held in high esteem. However, in an American society that worships youthfulness, health and vitality, the needs and concerns of senior citizens are often forgotten or ignored.

It is difficult to treat the elderly psychiatrically. Our usual treatment options of education and various forms of psychotherapy present new problems in this age group. Their character traits are more solidified and harder to change. Insight interpretations about the past are less appropriate. They are often scared and avoidant and do not follow up on suggestions. However, individual psychotherapy still has much to offer. Its supportive, non-judgmental milieu can give the older client an opportunity to vent and release pent-up frustration and anger. It encourages relationships and decreases isolation. It reduces the stress of separation and fulfills some of the senior citizen's emotional needs. It can diminish feelings of guilt, help place things in perspective, suggest alternatives and provide a degree of reality testing by acting not so much as the echo of conscience, but as the quiet voice of reason. It can foster optimism, reestablish self-confidence and encourage the development of new interests. It can help restore a sense of identity and direction.

With the elderly, we often have to make use of what I call the "social service function" of private practice psychiatry. Environmental manipulation, such as suggestions to downsize to independent living or assisted living, is often appropriate. I may suggest that they reach out to others such as family, neighbors and church members. I may tell them how they can obtain transportation from transport companies or make them aware of neighborhood resources such as Meals on Wheels, a senior center, a YMCA or hospital exercise group. Age-related physical changes that affect the action of drugs within the body must be kept in mind when prescribing medication for the elderly, to avoid the risk of side effects, drug interactions and toxic reactions. I always check with their family physicians or specialists before writing prescriptions for psychiatric medications. Medication compliance can also be a problem for this age group. They may not be able to afford the medication, they may forget to take the medication or they may try to fix a problem by taking more medication than is prescribed. A family member and/or the use of a labeled weekly pill dispenser may aid with compliance. Sally's story illustrates some of these issues.

Sally's Story

"My anxiety is mostly about my health. There is always something. Now, my eyes bother me a lot. I'm terribly worried about them. I keep thinking about my medical problems all the time. My balance also bothers me. It is terrible. I run into walls.

"My husband makes me nervous. He doesn't talk anymore at all. When I talk to him he cannot hear me, because he won't wear his hearing aid and he just says, "Huh huh?" He makes me so angry. I'm so bored. All he does is read the newspaper and watch TV. It makes me so nervous, just looking at him. If something happens, he won't even help me. He sees me struggle and won't even get up. If I ask him to do something, he always says that he will do it later. He is lazy.

"I have nobody to talk to. We just sit there and look at each other. I do my household chores just to have something to do. Otherwise I would go crazy. When I do the laundry, he says, 'why do you do the laundry so often?' Doesn't he know that I just need something to do? I could scream at him sometimes.

"Just thinking about all the doctors that I have to see makes me nervous. [In any one month, Sally sees five to eight physicians]. Just knowing that I have to sit three to four hours in their waiting rooms to see them upsets me and then some of them don't do anything except take my blood pressure and listen to my heart. They mostly just sit and type things into their computers. Do they even see me? I sometimes feel that they are just following me until I die. I'm very anxious. When something has to be done, I want to get it done with."

When I first met Sally, she complained of depression, which she felt was due to her frustration over multiple medical problems, including diabetes, hypothyroidism, hypertension and neuropathy in her legs. She was also losing the sight in her right eye as a result of damage done during cataract surgery. All of these physical issues had changed her quality of life in a negative way. Further history-taking revealed that she had also suffered multiple losses in the past three months: her sister had died, her girlfriend of over fifty years had died, her cat had died, her girlfriend's husband had died and her first husband had died. She was tearful, had diminished energy, difficulty falling asleep and lack of motivation. These historical events and her symptoms caused me to diagnose depression. However, her mental status examination further revealed a long history of anxiety, worry and avoidance, three of the cardinal symptoms of GAD. She admitted that she often felt tense, had heart palpitations, dizziness and queasiness in her stomach.

Sally grew up in Wassenberg, Germany, where she lived on a farm, babysat for her neighbors' children and took care of her nieces and nephews. She finished the eighth grade and then attended two years of "occupational school" for hairdressing. She attended this school one day a week and then apprenticed in a shop where the people were "terrible and mean" and used her to help in the kitchen. Her father died in World War II when she was sixteen. At age eighteen, she had a girlfriend who lived in Lanshut, Germany. The girlfriend was dating an American soldier who didn't have a car. His friend, Ray, also an American soldier, had one and volunteered to take them to see the girls. Ray kept coming back to Sally's home after that first trip. Her mother said, "What does he want all the time here?"

Sally and Ray dated for three years and then got married. When Sally was twenty-three, she and Ray moved to the United States and settled in his hometown in Massachusetts. Her mother asked, "Why do you want to go so far away?" and Sally answered, "I just want to go where he is." For a while she was happy. She enjoyed living in her new location. Ray's family was wonderful to her and included her in their lives. She attended night classes to improve her English and made a few friends. Things seemed to be going well. However, she soon realized that Ray was a playboy who constantly cheated on her. After seven years and numerous infidelities on his part, Sally filed for divorce.

Her older sister immigrated to Philadelphia and suggested that Sally move there and live with her and her husband. At first she slept on their couch and then she moved into a room in her brother-in-law's mother's house. While she was living there, a police officer named Harold stopped her for jaywalking. "Later, I realized that he just wanted to meet me," Sally said. "I was alone and lonely. He was very kind and helpful to me. He drove me around for different jobs. He would bring me things and try to please me. He took me to dinner and to the movies." After three years, they got married in his sister's house. They bought a duplex in Philadelphia. "Things were good for a while," she said. "Hal liked to travel and we took trips to Germany and Europe. We didn't talk much and I began to feel lonely. After about five years, I started to wonder if I had done the right thing marrying him. I do not know why I stayed. That was forty-four years ago."

Sally's Opinion of What Helped Her Anxiety

"Sometimes nothing helps me. I just go along with the program. Distracting myself helps me be less anxious. When I go to the casino, I'm calm. I do not have to think about anything. I forget everything and just play the slots. When my younger sister comes to visit from Germany, I'm calm. We have things to talk about and sometimes we go shopping at the mall. She understands me. She is also not well. She has leukemia. I worry about her and my niece's husband who has Parkinsonism. When I talk to people, it helps a little bit. When I come to see [Dr. Zal], it helps. [He listens] to me and I think that [he understands] what I mean."

My Opinion of What Helped Sally's Anxiety

My treatment of Sally was inconsistent, often interrupted due to intervening medical problems and hospitalizations for physical issues. Medication management was difficult. Initially, when Sally came to see me, she was on an antidepressant and a sleeping medication. She had been taking these

medications for over ten years. I spoke with her family physician and her
endocrinologist (for her diabetes) to make sure we were on the same page.

I questioned Sally about her diet. She said that her husband did all
the cooking and insisted on making meals high in carbohydrates. I spoke to
Harold about this and gave him a diabetic cookbook that I had discovered.
I also recommended that she increase her activity. I told her about a local
exercise program for senior citizens and asked her to register with a local
transportation service. I hoped that if she used this service, she could be
more independent and feel more in control.

Her physicians gave me medical clearance to slowly discontinue the
drug she was on and start Sally on another antidepressant in the morning
which I hoped would be more activating and increase her energy. Three
weeks later, she reported that she had no ill effects from discontinuing the
original medicine, had gone to the mall, visited her sister's grave and was
babysitting for her neighbor's cat. Sally's own cat had died three months
before and she had commented, "I get so attached to animals. When I lose
them, I'm a mess." I tucked this fact away in my mind for future reference.
Later in therapy, after again obtaining medical clearance, I added another
drug to her medication regime due to its antidepressant and antianxiety
potential.

I continued to encourage increased activity and social interaction. She
once told me that she used to love going to the pool to swim. I asked her to
walk outside more and go to her apartment complex pool, even if she just sat
under an umbrella and spoke to people. I told her about the availability of
books on tape and a free weekly movie at her local library. I called the local
hospital and got Sally information about their fitness classes for the elderly.
Unfortunately, she never followed through on these suggestions.

I realized that anxiety was a major problem for Sally. She often felt
jittery and sometimes had shortness of breath and palpitations when she
felt nervous. She was avoidant and worried a lot about different things. I
started her on an antianxiety agent twice a day. I had to reduce the dose to
once nightly due to the development of increased daytime sleepiness. This

reduction caused no improvement. Her sleepiness during the day continued. I taught her deep breathing exercises. Six months into therapy, I noticed that Sally was drifting to the left. She had been wobbly on her feet for two weeks and the day before had fallen while just standing in front of the mirror. I wondered if she had had a stroke.

She saw her family physician at my suggestion. He referred her to a neurologist, who sent her for an MRI of her head (negative), an EEG (electroencephalogram-brain wave study, also negative) and a sleep study. The sleep study showed probable restless leg syndrome and Sally was started on medication for this disorder. The neurologist felt that she had nerve damage due to her diabetes that was adding to her symptoms. He also noted that she had a slight weakness of her left arm and leg which made him wonder if she had not had a stroke.

During the next year, Sally was hospitalized and then went for rehabilitation to a nursing home for leg pain due to arterial disease (Sally smoked). She had a stent placed in her right leg, which clogged and she had to have a second surgery. She was hospitalized for dehydration and later a bowel resection, which left her with chronic diarrhea. Weight loss became an issue. Her walking became more and more unbalanced. She had to start using a walker for ambulation. She had surgery to remove a cancerous lesion from the side of her face. She complained of a chronic itch of the skin of her side and shoulder. "I do nothing but see doctors," she said. With each new medical issue and further physical decline, her anxiety, worry and depression increased and she fell back several steps emotionally. She started to have problems with short-term memory.

Medication compliance was also a problem. It was often hard to tell if she was taking her medications as prescribed: "It's getting confusing. I have thirteen pills to take." I spoke to Harold about this. He had no idea what medications she was taking. I suggested that they ask each doctor to write down the medications and how they wanted them taken and get a pill dispenser. I told him to take more responsibility overseeing Sally's medications. However, I was aware they often did not follow through on many of my suggestions. Once she said that she lost the information that I had written down for her. I started to realize that she was scared and although it was hard for her to admit, she felt more comfortable if her sister or husband accompanied her places. Neither she nor her husband liked change.

Both members of this couple were locked into their own limited routines. Harold read the paper, clicked the remote control, cooked, occasionally took Sally places and complained about what she did. Sally did the wash, some light housecleaning and complained about him. This was their marital pattern. They had few friends or acquaintances. One couple came over infrequently for dinner and to play cards. It was difficult to get Sally and Harold to budge out of this restricted way of life. As with most relationships, the difficulty is usually split fifty-fifty. It is not always the one making the most noise who is the biggest problem. As I previously mentioned, I believe that couples maintain equilibrium between them, like two people on a seesaw. If one changes even a little, the other has to change to maintain the equilibrium. My constant hope in doing therapy involving couples is that at least one will move a little in a positive direction.

Much of our time in individual psychotherapy was devoted to Sally's complaints about her husband. Her constant lament was, "He gets on my nerves. I'm just a mess." I asked her about her expectations of marriage. She said, "I guess I expect something else than I have. I want a better relationship. I want him to be more attentive to me. We argue a lot about money. He's very tight. Before my heart attack, I was always active. I want to do more on my own." It became clear that Sally resented her dependency on her husband in the last ten years but also realized on some level that she needed him. I asked her what she had liked about him when they first met. She said that she trusted him, he was very caring, he took her places and was always there for her. In these ways he was still the same. He was still there and still took her places. He drove her to the casino, to the mall and to her doctors' appointments. He cooked for her. She still trusted him.

She began to realize that he really had not changed that much. She agreed that he loved her and cared for her in his own way. For instance, he wouldn't allow her to use the car service, because he was worried that she would fall. He insisted on taking her shopping and on other outings himself. She was just feeling scared and more vulnerable and needed more from him. One day she admitted, "I look at my husband and realize that I'd be lost without him." I tried to help her look on the bright side and gain a positive perspective. In spite of all her physical problems, she lives at home and not in a nursing home, where she could be just sitting there staring at the walls. She is able to keep herself well-groomed and looking the best that she can. Sally's sister calls her and visits from Germany several times a year. She is not totally alone.

When I thought that I wasn't doing enough for Sally, I felt comforted by some wise advice that a supervisor gave me many years ago when I was a resident in psychiatry concerned that I wasn't doing enough for a client. She said to me, "Do you realize how much you mean to her just by being there?" I had never thought about that before. Through the years, I have tried to keep this aspect of my professional role in mind. This held true for my work with Sally. Coming to therapy gave her a chance to vent to someone she trusted and perhaps feel supported and not so alone. She went home feeling heard and valued. It was nice to see her smile when she came into the room. Whatever I did helped her and she appreciated my counsel.

Chapter 16

Holiday Anxiety

Happiness abounds during the holidays. We shop for presents, decorate our homes and offices, light the Christmas tree or Hanukkah menorah and prepare for our holiday dinners and festivities. In the media, cheerful people are shown celebrating together in harmony and love. However, the reality can be quite different. For many, particularly for the GAD client, feelings of increased anxiety can ruin the holidays. This is caused by time pressure and a need to please others. Anxiety symptoms may increase and many may start to feel out of control. For others there are even more intense feelings of depression caused by unfulfilled expectations and memories of those they have lost. Alcohol and drug use can increase. For some, these feelings are just a seasonal exacerbation. Many of my clients come into the therapy room during the holiday season and say, "I feel lousy. It's December and the holidays." The intensity of these feelings may subside by January. However, if we are not careful we can burn out and cross the threshold of the New Year feeling tense, exhausted, disgruntled and gloomy.

From Thanksgiving to the New Year, which is the busiest holiday period for most people, there is a medical model that can help as you try to deal with deadlines, complex family dynamics and an ever-expanding to-do list. The University of Texas MD Anderson Cancer Center tells cancer patients that "one of the best ways to promote your own health is to forget yourself and concentrate on helping others." When we help others, the body releases endorphins that can reduce pain, produce a sense of well-being and calm and relieve stress.[1] Spend some time giving to someone else, like volunteering for a local soup kitchen. Bringing a smile to someone can improve your mood, encourage relaxation and help you remember and spread the true, uplifting meaning of the holidays.

In this book, I have often mentioned that during times of anxiety you should make an effort to reduce isolation and self-pity. Instead, try reaching out to others and focus on the positive. Have hope and faith that it will all come together. My wish for you is that you will allow yourself to stop for a moment, take a deep breath in through your nose and let it out very slowly through pursed lips and start to refocus and relax in this way. Here are some other things that you can do to enjoy your holidays by keeping holiday anxiety and stress under control:

Have reasonable expectations of yourself and others. Perfection is an unrealistic goal. An anonymous writer once said, "Being happy doesn't mean that everything is perfect. It means that you've decided to look beyond the imperfections." There are many things that are not under our control. It is not really the external situation that causes stress but rather the way that we think about it and deal with the problem. Burnout can be defined as emotional and physical fatigue, usually based on unrealistically high expectations. People who have the most difficulty emotionally during the holiday season often ask too much from themselves and others. They tend to take on too much, give too much and expect too much. Lowering your expectations even 10 to 20 percent will decrease your chance for frustration and failure. Keep your expectations for the holiday season realistic and in line with your situation. Don't beat yourself up because you cannot afford everything on your children's wish lists. Instead of spending more money than you can afford, limit your purchases to stay within your budget.

It is not possible for other human beings to fulfill your needs 100 percent. If you expect a little less from others, you will be less disappointed. We cannot control others. We can only control what we think, feel and say.

Accept your relationships with your family for what they are. Try not to allow any already strained relationships to become worse during this season. Find the humor in situations.

Have practical time demands and try not to put yourself under time pressure. The main stress inducer of time management problems is having too much to do and too little control over the time and manner in which it is done. Trouble arises when we take on too much responsibility or expect to accomplish everything. This can be aggravated by the inability to establish boundaries between holiday planning and our other responsibilities in life. Set firm rules for the use of your time. You also need to allow time for yourself to rest or you will be too tired to enjoy the festivities. Dan Millman, former world champion athlete and author of *The Way of the Peaceful Warrior*, tells us, "When in haste, rest in the present. Take a deep breath and come back to the here and now."[2] Do what you can. Remember, your guests will not realize what you forgot or couldn't accomplish. Hopefully, they simply came to visit to spend time with you and your family.

Take care of yourself. Advice from Mayo Clinic physicians underlines the need for prevention and recommends making your physical and mental health a priority during the holiday season. They suggest avoiding anxiety by limiting yourself to responsibilities that you can handle. They tell you to ask for help from other family members and to draw boundaries on what you will do. Undercut money worries and head off financial pressure by making a realistic budget at the beginning of the season. They encourage you to not engage in disagreements with unpleasant family members and to say "no" when others try to talk you into taking on too much.[3] If you are alone, reach out to friends and others in the community. Perhaps through work or your religious affiliation you will find others in the same situation who may be willing to have a holiday dinner together. If this is not possible, at least reach out and try to talk to others, even if it is only by phone. Calling to wish people "Happy Holidays!" is a way to stay in touch and reduce your isolation. Check the local papers for holiday concerts and events that you can attend.

Give yourself time and permission to relax. Schedule time to recharge and drain off tension every day during the holidays. Stress can wear you out physically, lower your immunity and make you more prone to colds, flu and other illnesses. Take a break and go for a walk and/or continue your exercise program. Even fifteen minutes of alone time can help calm you down and clear your mind. Take a bubble bath, read a book, listen to music. Do your yoga workout or meditate. Remember to use your usual coping mechanisms. Refocus, do a deep breathing exercise or other relaxation technique, prioritize, practice self-talk or affirmations, make a to-do list. Practice mindfulness and focus on the here and now. Just close your eyes and imagine yourself in a beautiful, soothing place. Take care of your body and your physical condition. Get plenty of rest. Anxiety attacks can happen more often if you are sleep-deprived. A healthy diet can help. Avoid excessive caffeine and alcohol intake since alcohol can increase anxiety symptoms. Halt the salt and keep away from nicotine. Limit the amount of sweets and rich foods that you consume. Most of all, try to enjoy the festivities and have fun. This moment is part of your life. Don't waste it on unimportant things. Remember, like the holidays, this problem too shall pass.

Don't worry so much about what others think. People are usually not focusing on you as much as you assume. They probably are thinking about their own problems, hopes and insecurities. They probably will not notice if your house is not as spick-and-span as you wanted it to be. They don't have to like everything that you gave them as a gift. They don't have to approve of your dress, your actions or your choice of dessert. Do not give others so much power over you. Recall former First Lady Eleanor Roosevelt's words: "No one can make you feel inferior without your consent." Not everyone has to like what you do. Do you like everything that they do? Try to follow what author and spiritual leader Don Miguel Ruiz suggested: "Don't take everything personally. Nothing others do is because of you. What others say and do is a projection of their own reality, their own dreams. When you are immune to the opinions and actions of others, you won't be a victim of needless suffering."[4]

Seek contentment, not happiness. Many people seek happiness. Happiness is a fleeting emotion. No one is happy every minute of his or her life. Savor it when it appears, but do not expect it to be a constant. I think that a more reasonable goal for us all, particularly during periods of stress like the holidays, is contentment. Acceptance of yourself as human, warts and all, is a great pathway to feeling better. Shuck the anger, guilt and negative feelings. They only use up energy that you can use more constructively. As an osteopathic physician, I try to keep in mind Andrew Taylor Still's philosophy that we should focus on the whole person.[5] I suggest that your goal during the next holiday season be to allow yourself to move toward contentment in as many aspects of your life as possible. Focus on gratitude for what you do have. If you can be at peace with yourself, the people in your life, the hand that you have been dealt and the road that you have chosen, you will be less anxious, feel more in control of your world and ultimately feel happier more often.

Ask for Help. Accept the fact that you cannot do it all. Ask the other members of your household to do some of the tasks or help out in some way. Sometimes people do not volunteer but will lend a hand if you ask. If they do help you, don't criticize the way they do it even if it is not done your way or less than perfect. Ask people to bring something for the holiday meal. If all else fails and you do get anxious or depressed, accept that you are human. Don't be angry at yourself. If the symptoms continue after the holidays, seek professional help and see your physician. Don't be afraid or ashamed to ask for help. It is available. Remember, even average people react to stress. Bring a friend with you to a holiday party to provide support. If you are prone to anxiety attacks, let a friend know that you may be calling for verbal support.

I hope these suggestions are helpful to you during holiday seasons. Many people worry about giving the perfect gift, having the perfect party or wearing the perfect outfit. Perhaps we would be better off thinking less about how much money we spend and rely, as I have mentioned before, on the wisdom of author Leo Buscaglia when he said, "Too often we under-estimate the power of touch, a smile, a kind word, a listening ear, an honest compliment, or the smallest act of caring, all of which have the potential to turn a life around."[6] When in doubt as to what perfect gift to give another, just give of yourself. That is what we really want from each other. Tell your family and friends that you love and appreciate them. Sharing this message with others is the best gift they can receive.

Conclusion

The Road
to Contentment

Many clients come to therapy seeking happiness. Life is chaotic, filled with stress and difficult roadblocks. Illness and tragedy abound. Loss is inevitable. Happiness is fleeting. No one is constantly happy. Instead, seek contentment. A content person is a calmer person. Acceptance of yourself as human, along with your imperfections, is a great way to feel better. In therapy, my goal is to allow patients to move toward contentment in as many aspects of their lives as possible. You will be less anxious if you can be at peace with yourself, the people in your life, the hand that you have been dealt and the road that you have chosen. You will feel more in control of your world and ultimately be happier more often.

Andrew Weil, MD, physician, author, natural-remedy guru and champion of integrative medicine, was interviewed about his book, *Spontaneous Happiness*, by a reporter for *The Philadelphia Inquirer*. He said, "I think most people don't have the right conception of what happiness is. They think being happy is to get something they don't have. The best thing to work for is contentment, which is an inner sense of fulfillment that's relatively independent of external circumstances."[1] Physician and Indian Yoga Master Swami Sivananda said it well when he proclaimed, "There is no end to craving. Hence, contentment alone is the best way to happiness. Therefore, acquire contentment."[2]

We come into adulthood believing that we will be happy once we achieve the cultural goals of adult success: graduating from the right school, marrying the perfect spouse, having beautiful children and securing a good job paying a large salary, offering upward mobility and enabling us to have a large house in the suburbs. These achievements, although they can offer us great moments of joy and pleasure, do not stay at this level of intensity forever. Author and University of California psychology professor Sonja Lyubomirsky in her book, *The Myths of Happiness*, calls these "false promises."[3] She suggests that we look beyond these fantasies of success and happiness and focus our perspective, expectations and attitude on wiser choices such as relationships, learning, challenging ourselves and reaching out to others.[4] Here are some guidelines that I share with clients that may help you move in the direction of contentment:

Take a problem-solving approach to life. If someone were to ask me which of the ten steps presented in this book is the most important, I would say the eighth step, "Take Action." This is one of the best ways to stop the cycle of anxiety and worry. Be proactive and take charge of your life. Ask for what you want. Your pride and a fear of rejection may often stand in your way of doing this. People cannot read your mind. Do not assume that we all think alike. We have all been brought up by different parents and raised in different emotional environments. At work, where your boss focuses on the bottom line, they may not give you a raise unless you ask for it. Don't sit around and hope others will just automatically know what you want and give it to you. Be active in reaching out to achieve your goals.

Speak with a mentor who can give you a different point of view. If you have financial worries, talk to your accountant and a financial advisor and find out the truth of your situation. Rather than feeling weighed down by health or other worries, get the information that you need to put things in perspective, set you on a more positive road and allow you to feel more in control. In dealing with people, good communication skills also involve examining your assumptions before you respond or act.

An important line from step eight is, "Rather than feeling over-whelmed, prioritize and get the job done one task at a time." If your inbox on your desk is piled high with things to do, the best approach, rather than giving in to hopelessness, is to set your priorities and complete one item at a time. This also holds true for other things that cause you anxiety and worry and inspire avoidance.

A client of mine, James, used a unique metaphor to describe how he sees this process and deals with his "stack of concerns." He wrote, "Visually, the anxieties I've experienced are a washboard. Not 'like' a washboard, but actually a washboard. A washboard is made up of a frame surrounding a solid surface of ripples, stacked one upon another. Each ripple may represent separate concerns, worries, issues to be dealt with and fears. But again, it is a solid surface of ripples, not single ripples that can be removed singly to flatten the surface—to make things calm and peaceful. Each ripple, each concern, is interconnected, part of a union of ripples; when my anxieties are not looked at as their separate parts, the whole is quite overwhelming. Wielding a hammer to flatten these ripples, one at a time—focusing on dealing with each worry and fear and issue—smoothing things out, is a chore that takes a lot of effort and concentration. This is especially true when the stack of concerns is 'if this happens, then that happens, which affects this.' And so on. These are ripples on a washboard."

Use your energy for growth rather than trying to change that which cannot be changed. Evaluate your needs and expectations. Know what you want and go for it. Many people do not progress in life, because they do not know what they want. Challenge yourself. Ask yourself what you wanted to do before your present responsibilities carried you away. Did you want to start a business, get a degree or learn a new skill? Do you want to meet new people, go to the gym, begin a new hobby or finally read some of those books on your shelf? Dream and take action. Decide what you really want. Make a commitment to your goals and then work at making them a reality. Setting goals and working toward them consistently and patiently often engenders success.

Have realistic expectations of yourself and others. Perfection is an unrealistic goal. There are many things that are not under our control. Make peace with who you are and believe in yourself. Accept your own limitations and accept others as they are. Interpersonal relationships are not always easy. You cannot change other people. You can only take responsibility for your own actions and your 50 percent of the interaction. If you expect everyone to be perfect, you will be constantly frustrated and probably alone.

The serenity prayer, written by theologian Reinhold Niebuhr and utilized in the Alcoholics Anonymous Twelve Step Program, is about acceptance. It tells us that we cannot control everything in our lives. We need to develop the wisdom to know which things we have to let go and which things we can control. It tells us to learn to live a healthy lifestyle one day at a time, manage our expectations and accept and adapt to what is. This is good advice by which to live.

Reduce feelings of shame and guilt. These heavy emotions can be a roadblock to success and cause much emotional pain. Many of the people I see for treatment tend to be too hard on themselves and blame themselves 100 percent. Most problems in relationships are fifty-fifty, regardless of who is making the most noise. Why does it always have to be entirely your fault? You are accountable only for your fifty percent. An unknown author encouraged, "Delight in yourself; relax; lighten up. Let go of shame and fear. The whole picture is perfect, and perfectly okay."

Don't worry so much about what others think. Many of my clients with anxiety say that they're worried about what other people think about them. My answer is, "People are usually not focusing on you as much as you assume. You are not the center of the universe. They probably are concentrating on their own issues. They don't have to like everything that you do or say. Do not give others so much power over you. You are allowed to have your own opinions and your own preferences." Not everyone has to approve of what you do.

Find ways to blow off steam. Holding feelings inside will eventually cause you either emotional or physical problems. In therapy, people learn the value of sharing their feelings, talking through their problems and verbalizing their concerns. We all need someone to listen to us sometimes. John Gray, PhD, made a good point in his book, *Men Are From Mars, Women Are From Venus*, about how males and females deal with stress differently. He says that men become quiet and go into their caves to mull things over and problem solve. Women, on the other hand, seek out someone whom they can trust and talk about their problems. They have to empty the bucket. It you interfere with this task, they can get annoyed.[5] This premise is true. However, it is not just women who can benefit by talking about their problems. It may take them longer to open up, but men also will feel better if they let it all out in a safe and accepting environment.

My hope is that if people can learn to talk it out in therapy, they will eventually do the same outside of the therapy room. This requires trust and selectivity. Even though I encourage clients to share their thoughts and feelings, this does not mean that they should do it equally with everyone. It is not a good idea to tell your boss that you have no respect for him. Your spouse or significant other is a human being. Even sharing with him or her requires tact and respect for his or her feelings. When you want to share, keep in mind that some people are limited in their ability to deal with anger and criticism. Some will just throw your words back at you and be angry. If the people in your life are limited, find friends, relatives, mentors, clergy or counselors who may be better equipped to hear you out.

If you cannot always talk your feelings out, find other ways to relieve your frustration and excess aggressive energy. You can easily learn relaxation techniques. Exercise works for many and is one of the best ways to reduce nervousness and stress. Activity, whether it is a brisk walk or an hour at the gym, can be helpful to reduce anxiety and worry. Sex and affection are great stress busters. Sex causes the brain to release endorphins, which are chemicals that can reduce feelings of pain and anxiety. A simple hug can do wonders to calm your nerves. Water activities can be soothing. Why not try swimming, rowing a boat or canoeing? Involvement in an active sport such as bowling, tennis or ping pong can help reduce tension. Video games may distract you but they may not offer the same benefit as a sport or activity.

Get more involved in the world. This is one of the best ways to reduce isolation, which can interfere with good mental health. Staying in your own dark, self-centered world will only increase your anxiety and magnify the negatives. Let the light come in. Give back and reach out to—and invest more in—others. It will help you stop thinking about your own problems. It will also help you gain perspective. You will realize that you are not alone. Others have similar problems and perhaps yours are not the worst. Often answering the question, "What do you want to add to your life?" will open up a plethora of possibilities and get you thinking proactively. Even reading a daily newspaper is a way to invest yourself more in the world outside. Charity and volunteer work can give you much back and increase self-esteem. Doing something that you like, outside the house, will help you meet new people with common interests. Take a class, join a hiking club or volunteer for your church choir. All of these things can help reduce your isolation and add to your sense of happiness and contentment.

It is not just GAD that will be helped by this approach. I feel that the key to a successful life overall is to stay involved and maintain a passion for work and other projects. Take charge of your life and don't ever be without a goal. Continue to learn and grow. Become creative and productive. Be active and allow your life to really be an adventure. Have fun. We all need something to look forward to when we get up in the morning.

Pay attention to relationships. Don't take people for granted. Remember to keep in contact with your friends, parents, siblings and extended family. Otherwise, they will think that you are not interested and that you want to be alone. You must consciously and consistently work on relationships that are important to you. Even if you are busy, perhaps it would help to remember to call each of your friends and family members at least once per month. The best way to make a friend is to show an interest in him or her. Family members and friends are not perfect. Sometimes it is best not to take their words or behavior at face value. Focus on their good points. Do they outweigh their negative attributes?

Don't close the door on relationships with those you love. Each interaction can be a new beginning. In the long run, it is these emotional bonds that we form with parents, children and friends that sustain us and provide quality in our lives. What changes as we get older is not what we actually know or actually have but the nuances that give new meaning to things. What changes is perspective: We gain an ability to see the whole picture. A new clarity develops about what is really important in life. As you age, you gain a new appreciation of good health, freedom from emotional and physical pain and meaningful relationships, which linger long after material goals are reached and money is spent.

Often we do not reach out or are offended if people do not reciprocate an invitation. Remember, some people are not callers or party givers. Do not stand on ceremony. Don't let pride or fear of rejection stand in your way of reaching out. If they are happy to hear from you when you call them, that is all that matters. It doesn't matter who called first. Ask for what you want. It is not a guarantee of success but people cannot read your mind. Do not assume that everyone thinks the same way. Verbalize your feelings, concerns and needs. Mexican author Don Miguel Ruiz shared wisdom when he said, "Don't make assumptions. Find the courage to ask questions and to express what you really want. Communicate with others as clearly as you can to avoid misunderstandings, sadness and drama. With just this one agreement, you can completely transform your life."[6]

Focus on the Positive. We all have basic physiological needs for nourishment and rest. However, we also have other important needs. These include acceptance, approval, honesty, trust, hope, respect, dignity and freedom from pain. Affection, tenderness, intimacy and love are paramount to a full existence. Being close to another human being with whom you can share your secrets and your life can add another dimension. Intimacy is a very basic human need. We all need to love and be loved. Sex is part of the equation, but so is physical touch, kind words and companionship. We all need comforting and nurturing at times. We need to know that someone cares. Praise can help a person to blossom. A compliment can raise self-esteem.

One of the reasons that individual therapy works for many is that it can offer acceptance and point out the positive aspects of the individual. The counselor-client relationship is a strong therapeutic tool. Therapy cannot totally make up for the things that you did not obtain in childhood. It cannot completely fill or reverse the void often left by earlier unfulfilled needs for love or nurturing. But it can give you the support, encouragement and acceptance that you did not receive when you were young. If a counselor can help you to feel better about yourself, it will go a long way toward balancing the deficit.

Balance! This is the magic word that best describes how to lead a content, successful and fulfilled life. This wisdom is so easy to give and so hard to put into practice. A work-life balance is important. In this day and age, we work long hours and come home tired. We run from pillar to post, from office to home and seek gratification in material rewards. When does the fun begin? When do our real lives begin? If we are lucky, one day we wake up and start to look at the big picture. We realize that this day *is* life.

Hopefully, you can start to broaden your horizons and add new and interesting bricks to the foundation of work that has been the majority of your life thus far. Perhaps you can start to pay more attention to personal relationships, increase your level of intimacy, start a hobby, volunteer and exercise. In other words, create a better balance in your life between work and play. If you are lucky, you will learn the lesson of love and its central position in a life of meaning. Elizabeth Kubler-Ross said, "Love has nothing to do with knowledge, education or power; it is beyond behavior. It is also the only gift in life that is not lost. Ultimately, it is the only thing we can really give. In a world of illusions, a world of dreams and emptiness, love is the source of truth."[7]

Take Care of Yourself. Your emotional and physical health is important. Pay attention to the quality of your life. Take time for yourself. Develop interests and friendships that are meaningful to you. Make use of as many techniques as you can to relax and rest. Take care of your body. Watch your diet. Pay attention to nutrition and rest. Slow down a little. Leave time for leisure and fun. Exercise to work off aggressive energy. Take time for relaxation. Perhaps a decompression zone between work and home will help you deal with stress better. Lighten the situation with laughter. Make time in your busy life for fun. You don't have to travel to a faraway amusement park to allow yourself to relax. It is okay to act a little childish at times, even at home. Freudian psychoanalysis calls this "regression in the service of the ego."[8] It allows you to reconstitute. You may need some privacy and time to yourself. Get away from it all at times by scheduling a long weekend or other time off. Get medical treatment early before physical problems escalate.

Early in my residency training, I was given advice by a supervisor: "If you are going to take care of others, make sure that you take care of yourself. Eat three meals a day, take breaks and get enough rest. This is not selfishness. It is self-preservation." These are good recommendations for anyone who has to deal with stress, regardless of the source.

Have your own life. Don't just rely on others for your happiness. Many people live with the illusion that there is a wonderful other person out there who will make you happy and fulfill all your needs. This is obviously not true. That is not really the responsibility of the people in your life. Any good marriage or successful relationship must include an "us" based on common interests and goals, as well as room for two independent people who have separate interests and hobbies. A significant other can add to the quality of your life but shouldn't be your entire existence.

Have A Belief System. In this chaotic world it is helpful to have something to hold on to. A belief system, which is something that either an individual or group of people believe in, can fulfill this need. The most common is a religious belief system. Respected Christian minister and spiritual advisor Billy Graham has said, "If I didn't have spiritual faith, I would be a pessimist. But I am an optimist. I've read the last page in the Bible. It's going to turn out all right."[9] Any group association can offer feelings of comfort, security and belonging. This can be a scientific belief system, which is based on observation and reasoning. It can even be something political, such as a viewpoint or faith in a political party or ideology that connects you to others and gives you strength. Teenagers get this same sense of security by being part of a group. A client of mine spoke of "tribalism" or a feeling of "us people."

In therapy, we want to know what gives a person's life meaning and hope and who or what will help them cope during difficult times. For those who believe, religion and spiritual beliefs can prevent self-harm or harm to others. They can be a roadblock to suicide. Generally a belief system refers to the fundamental assumptions, ideas and expectations rather than documented proof. Freud regards God as an illusion based on the infantile need for a powerful father figure. However, religious beliefs help many feel more secure. For several of the clients illustrated in this book, spirituality has served as an important and helpful element in their lives.

One of my clients, Clarence, answered the question, "My anxiety is…?" by explaining, "My anxiety is influenced by the behavior and reactions of other people. If my environment is disrupted by others having an outburst of anger, I am enveloped by feelings of anxiety and doubt, which can take days to quiet down." Clarence lived in fear of upsetting his wife and his mother, who could both be demanding. To keep his "environment" calm and anger free, he spent a lot of energy walking on eggshells and trying to please others. In spite of natural talent and a good work ethic, his need to please authority and his low self-esteem kept him from asking for advancement at his job. It also kept him from going back to school to get a college degree that would have helped his progress. "I feel the need to solve others' problems before taking care of my own," he said. "When the time comes for me to take care of my own problems or priorities, I am too exhausted." Several years ago, at his wife's insistence, he and his family joined a Mormon church and got involved in the community. This religious affiliation, along with individual psychotherapy, has given him a more solid footing. It helps him feel better about himself and gives him a sense of contentment and belonging. He is more willing to speak out, express his desires and set limits where necessary.

Attending some sort of worship, even occasionally, can offer emotional support and a feeling of connection. A 2010 National Med Poll showed that 79 percent of healthcare professionals believed that a religious faith can have a positive impact on a patient's outcome.[10] A Pew Research Center study showed that attending religious services helps increase happiness in retirement.[11]

Ask for Help. Anxious people often feel that they have to handle every aspect of their lives themselves. This is not true. Sometimes even the strongest people need someone to talk to—someone who can offer sustenance and light the way. We all need support at times. Asking for help does not make you weak. For every life problem there are resources to be tapped for information and suggestions. Then you can decide what is best for you. At every stage of life, mentors are available. Reach out and form these helpful relationships. Parenting is a hard job; just sharing with other parents can make the process easier. Joining a play group or going out socially with other couples who have children the same age can be helpful.

Being a caregiver may drain you emotionally and physically. Always remember that community resources are available. Know your limits and reach out for aid. Help is available if you suffer from emotional pain and have symptoms of mental illness. Just pick up the phone. At various stages of life, we all ask, "Why didn't someone tell me?" The answer probably is because we did not ask.

I hope that reading this book has given you a new perspective on GAD. If you have been anxious all your life, regardless of your present age, the client vignettes included here are proof that you are not alone. I hope that you have identified with some of these people and learned something from them. I hope that their experiences resonated with you and helped you realize that although you are feeling "nervous," you are not going to lose control. You are not going to go crazy. Something terrible is not going to happen. You are not going to die. You are just feeling anxious!

As I have said, anxiety often presents with physical symptoms and overlaps with other emotional and physical problems. Please get these checked out by an appropriate physician. However, even if all the work-ups are negative, realize that GAD is a real medical illness that can be treated and helped but no one can make it go away forever. It is part of your genetic makeup—part of your very being. Nonetheless, there is much that you can do to help yourself feel more in control. Medication is useful at times. Individual psychotherapy, cognitive-behavioral therapy and other therapies can also help some people feel better. Diet and exercise are important. Do not give up. Take a proactive approach, because there is hope. Take control of your anxiety, rather than letting it control you. Work on reducing your unrealistic worry. Avoid avoidance.

But most of all, seek contentment. A calmer person is a content person who is comfortable with him or herself and the world. Things are not black and white. A proper perspective can help you attain harmony. Life is a gift that offers an abundance of riches, but not constantly. We have to have the right attitude, the right perspective and reasonable expectations.

At times of doubt, try saying to yourself, "Don't worry. It will all work out." Remember what novelist, journalist and Pulitzer Prize winner Anna Quindlen says in her book, *A Short Guide to a Happy Life*: "Life is made up of moments of small pieces of glittering mica in a long stretch of gray cement."[12] Seek contentment and not constant happiness. Be optimistic. Look for the small sparkling moments of life; they are there and you can find them if you focus. Be glad and grateful when you see the warm glow of the lights.

I am optimistic that the suggestions and therapies discussed in this book will help you be calmer and less nervous. However, be aware that they are just suggestions. Please talk to your own physician, mental health worker or psychiatrist about your problems. I believe that each person deserves an individualized treatment plan. These professionals can tell you which strategies will be most helpful for you. Good luck. But most of all, I wish you contentment and good emotional and physical health. As I get older, I begin to better understand the phrase, "we are all in this together." Regardless of our individual qualities and personalities, inside we are all just human beings with the same needs and desires. In the course of a lifetime, we all go through similar trials and tribulations and have parallel concerns about relationships, money, health matters and the future.

Life is short. This is not a dress rehearsal. We only pass this way once. Learn to love and appreciate the journey of existence. Be kind to yourself and to each other. I sincerely hope that you will also continue to reduce your anxiety, relax and enjoy your life.

Acknowledgments

My first book, *Panic Disorder: The Great Pretender*, changed my professional life and my professional identity. Prior to this, I was a general psychiatrist who saw all types of what we then called "neurotic" and "psychotic" clients. With this book, I soon found myself receiving numerous referrals for the diagnosis of panic disorder. My practice began to expand in that direction. Many of the referred clients really had generalized anxiety disorder and not panic disorder. As time went by, I started seeing many clients who suffered from various other anxiety disorders.

I was fortunate enough to be selected as a speaker by the Upjohn Pharmaceutical Company, whose drug indicated for panic disorder had just come onto the market. For about two years, I spoke all over Pennsylvania. I also spoke on anxiety disorder topics at various osteopathic state, national and medical conventions and meetings. Writing became more than a hobby. It was now an avocation. I began to see myself as a psychiatrist, a writer, a lecturer and an editor.

I gave the third draft of this book to two friends: William White, a true renaissance man with a multifaceted background, and Stephen Parker, a former college English professor, writer, poet and businessman. Steve returned the manuscript with a note that read: "This promises to be the best book I've read that deals with GAD…Primarily, the appeal and usefulness of the book come from your [author's] voice, which [is] unusually empathetic and confident, but kindly and caring...you present the disorder at a level which can be understood and ingested by virtually anyone. Additionally, the structure you've chosen—general overview of patient, patient's view, your view and then therapeutic results—is very effective and interesting." When I read this note, I knew that I was moving in the right direction. It helped me to keep going in my writing. I am thankful to Bill and Steve for their time and editorial work but most of all for their friendship.

A special note of thanks goes to my clients. During my forty-three years of being in solo practice in psychiatry, for the most part they have given me their respect and their trust. They have shared their problems, their feelings and their secret thoughts with me. I have gained much pleasure in seeing many of them improve and grow emotionally during our time together. I am pleased that I could help them but they also have added much to my life. Even after all these years, I still enjoy working with people and their problems and seeing my clients progress.

The individuals whose stories you read here signed releases giving me permission to use their psychiatric histories or life stories, as well as their medical records. All of the clients' names have been changed.

Special thanks go to Karl Rickels, MD, for writing the foreword to this book. I have known Karl professionally for more than thirty years. He is a well-known and well-thought-of physician who is the Stuart and Emily B.H. Mudd Professor of Human Behavior and professor of Psychiatry at the University of Pennsylvania and founder of the University of Pennsylvania Private Practice Research Group. In the early 1980s, I was lucky enough to do some research for Karl at my office in Bala Cynwyd, Pennsylvania. I was an osteopathic physician and a psychiatrist. He was a big name in research and psychiatry. He was kind enough to include my name along with other minor investigators in two papers that he had published in international journals.

When I finished writing the third draft of this book, I decided to send it out for publication. However, this time I chose to find a literary agent rather than do all the work myself. I was very lucky: I contacted Anne G.

Devlin of the Max Gartenberg Literary Agency in Yardley, Pennsylvania. Anne responded that she would very much like the opportunity to represent my work.

Anne helped me tweak my book proposal. I signed a contract with her on July 28, 2012. Within eight days, I received my first offer. I received a second offer in three weeks time. Anne had done a good job. Thank you, Anne G. Devlin, for your diligence and your faith in me.

Many thanks to the staff at New Horizon Press for their help and positive approach to my manuscript. My appreciation goes to Dr. Joan S. Dunphy, Publisher; Caroline Russomanno, Assistant Editor/Publicist; Charley Nasta, Production Editor; and JoAnne Thomas, Vice President of Finance and Marketing, for all their hard work.

I have dedicated this book to my wife, Alice J. Zal, DO, FACOFP, a family physician, with all my love to a very special lady. In spite of all her responsibilities and time pressures, she has always been there for me, caring and loving. I thank her for reading the third draft of this book and for her copy editing and editorial suggestions. We will soon be married forty-nine years. This is unusual in this day and age. Many times, we go to functions and are in the minority of people there with their first spouses. I was twenty-three and Alice was twenty-two when we got married. We have been through a lot together. We have grown up together. We raised two children, lost another child and went through school with each other. We worked in the same office for ten years and have been through a lot, professionally and otherwise. We share the same values and the same goals. Like any marriage, we have our "stuff," but the love is still there and has grown stronger through the years. Alice is also smart, talented and beautiful. What more can I ask for? I am glad that she is still by my side and in my life.

—*H Michael Zal*

Helpful Resources

American College of Osteopathic Psychiatrists and Neurologists
acn-aconp@msn.com
28595 Orchard Lake Rd., Suite 200
Farmington Hills, MI 48334
Phone: (248) 553-6207
Fax: (248) 553-0818
Website: http://www.acn-aconp.org

American Psychiatric Association
apa@psych.org
1000 Wilson Boulevard
Suite 1825
Arlington, VA 22209
Phone: 1-888-357-7924
Website: www.psych.org

American Psychoanalytic Association
info@apsa.org
309 East 49th Street
New York, New York 10017-1601
Phone: (212) 752-0450
Fax: (212) 593-0571
Website: www.apsa.org

The Anxiety Self-Help Homepage
http://www.healthyplace.com/anxiety-panic/articles/
anxiety-self-help-homepage/

The Anxiety and Depression Association of America
www.adaa.org
8701 Georgia Ave. #412
Silver Spring, MD 20910
Phone: 1-240.485.1001

Anxieties.com – Free anxiety self-help site

AnxietyTribe: An Online Anxiety Support Community
http://www.anxietytribe.com

The Association for Applied Psychophysiology and Biofeedback (formerly
the Biofeedback Society of America)
http://www.aapb.org
10200 W. 44th Avenue
Suite 304
Wheat Ridge, CO 80033-2840
Phone: 1-800-477-8892 / 303-422-8436
Fax: 303-422-8894
E-mail: AAPB@resourcenter.com

Association for Cognitive and Behavioral Therapies
http://www.abct.org
305 7th Avenue, 16th Fl., New York, NY 10001
Phone (212) 647-1890
ABCT's directory of certified therapists:
http://www.abct.org/Members/?m=findTherapist&fa=FT_Form&nolm=1.

Canadian Mental Health Association
www.cmha.ca

CounsellingResource.com: Allows you to take psychological self-tests, check symptoms of common mental health disorders, look up medication and compare types of counseling and psychotherapy.

Esperanza Magazine: Hope to cope with anxiety and depression.
Kelbrish Publishing, Inc.
P.O. Box 59
Buffalo, New York 14205
866-740-4673
www.hopetocope.com

Generalized anxiety disorder – MayoClinic.com
www.mayoclinic.com/health/generalized-anxiety-disorder/DS00502

Generalized anxiety disorder symptoms – Psych Central
psychcentral.com/disorders/sx24.htm

Maum Meditation- visit www.maum.org to find a center near you.

MedlinePlus
http://www.nlm.nih.gov/medlineplus

Mental Health America
www.MentalHealthAmerica.net

Mind Publications: Anxiety & Panic Attacks in Medical Patients
http://www.mindpub.com/art537.htm

National Alliance on Mental Illness
www.nami.org

National Association of Cognitive-Behavioral Therapists
http://nacbt.org
P.O. Box 2195
203 Three Springs Drive, Suite 4
Weirton, WV 26062
Phone: 1-800-853-1135

National Institute of Anxiety and Stress, Inc.
http://www.ConquerAnxiety.com
900 E. Pecan St., Ste. 300-305
Pflugerville, Texas 78660
Phone: 1-888-209-4061

The National Institute of Mental Health
www.nimh.nih.gov/index.shtml
9000 Rockville Pike
Bethesda, Maryland 20892
Phone: 1-301-496-4000

NIMH Mental Health Medications
http://www.nimh.nih.gov/health/publications/mental-health-medications/
complete-index.shtml

TAPIR: The Anxiety Panic Internet Resource
www.algy.com/anxiety/index.php

About the Author

H Michael Zal, DO, FACN, FAPA Dist, has been a psychiatrist for over forty years. He is currently in private practice in Norristown, Pennsylvania and a clinical professor in the Department of Psychiatry at the Philadelphia College of Osteopathic Medicine. He is board certified, a Fellow of the American College of Neurology and Psychiatry and a Distinguished Life Fellow of the American Psychiatric Association. He is Editor-in-Chief of *The Journal of the Pennsylvania Osteopathic Medical Association.*

Dr. Zal is a graduate of the University of Pennsylvania and the Philadelphia College of Osteopathic Medicine. He completed a three-year Psychiatric Fellowship sponsored by the National Institute of Mental Health at the Philadelphia Mental Health Clinic and Haverford State Hospital.

He is emeritus at the Belmont Center for Comprehensive Treatment, Philadelphia, Pennsylvania, and served as president of their medical staff. He was chairman of the Psychiatric Service at Metropolitan Hospital in Philadelphia for ten years and a member of the University of Pennsylvania Private Practice Research Group. He was also on the staff of Charter-Fairmount Institute, Mercy Suburban Hospital and the Medical College of Pennsylvania.

Dr. Zal received the Albert Einstein Healthcare Foundation Physicians' Award for Excellence and the Practitioner of the Year Award from the Philadelphia Psychiatric Society, for outstanding character, dedication and commitment to patient care.

He is a lecturer, medical writer and editor on mental health topics with numerous published articles to his credit. He was the winner of the Eric W. Martin Memorial Award, presented by the American Medical Writers Association, for outstanding writing and the Frances Larson Memorial Award for excellence. Dr. Zal is also the author of *Panic Disorder: The Great Pretender* (Da Capo/Perseus Press), *The Sandwich Generation: Caught Between Growing Children and Aging Parents* (Da Capo/Perseus Press) and *Dancing With Medusa: A Life In Psychiatry: A Memoir* (Authorhouse).

He is active in the community and has served as President of the Welsh Valley Civic Association, as a member of the Board of Directors of the Variety Club of Philadelphia and President of the Board of Managers of the Associated Alumni of the Central High School of Philadelphia.

Dr. Zal is married to Alice J. Sheflin Zal, DO, FACOFP, a family physician who practiced in Norristown, Pennsylvania and was President of the Pennsylvania Osteopathic Medical Association. They currently live in Lansdale, Pennsylvania and Atlantic City, New Jersey. They have two children, Michelle J. Dubin, RN, MSN, CPUR, and Fredrick H. Zal, who is a registered architect, a son-in-law, Steven Dubin, a CFO at a landscape architectural firm, and two grandchildren, Daniel Cory Dubin and Rebecca Haley Dubin.

Notes

Introduction

1. Søren Kierkegaard, *The Concept of Anxiety* (Princeton, New Jersey: Princeton University Press, 1953).

2. D.W. Goodwin, *Anxiety* (New York: Oxford University Press, 1986) 10, 51-78.

3. Jacob Mendes Da Costa, "On irritable heart: A clinical study of a form of functional cardiac disorder and its consequences" *American Journal of Medical Sciences*, Vol. 61 (1871), 17-52.

4. Sigmund Freud, *A General Introduction to Psychoanalysis* (New York: Permabooks, 1958), 405.

5. M.T. Eaton and M.H. Peterson, "Introduction to dynamic psychiatry" *Psychiatry Medical Outline Series*, 2nd ed. (New York: Medical Examination Publishing Co., 1969), 11-14.

6. Jennifer Warner, "Anxiety Often Missed in Elderly: More Older Adults Affected by Anxiety Disorders Than Depression," *WebMD* (May 22, 2006) http://www.webmd.com/anxiety-panic/guide/20061101/anxiety-missed-elderly.

A GAD Case History: Paul's Story

1. Nancy L. Mace, MA, and Peter V. Rabins, MD, MPH, *The 36-Hour Day: A Family Guide to Caring for Persons with Alzheimer Disease* (New York: Grand Central Publishing, 2001).
2. Tyler Perry, "An 11-year-old I Know," *Newsweek*, (December 5, 2011) 26.

Chapter 1   Step 1: Stop

1. G. Carey and H. Gottesman, "Twin and family studies of anxiety, phobic and obsessive-compulsive disorder," *Anxiety: New Research and Changing Concepts*, D.F. Klein and J. Rabin, eds. (New York: Raven Press, 1981).
2. S.M. Paul and P. Skolnick, "Benzodiazepine receptors and psycho-pathological states; Towards the neurobiology of anxiety," *Anxiety: New Research and Changing Concepts*, D.F. Klein and J. Rabin, eds. (New York: Raven Press, 1981).
3. R. Hoehn-Saric and D.R. McLeod, eds., *Biology of Anxiety Disorders* (Washington, DC: American Psychiatric Press, Inc., 1993), 1-2, 61-63.

Chapter 3   Step 3: Refocus

1. www.Learn-About-Alcoholism.com.
2. Gilda Berger, *Alcoholism and the Family* (New York: Franklin Watts Publisher, 1993).
3. Viktor Frankl, *Man's Search for Meaning* (New York: Washington Square Press, 1984).
4. www.quotationspage.com.

Chapter 4   Step 4: Lower Your Expectations

1. www.ThinkExist.com.
2. Fritz Perls, *Gestalt Therapy Verbatim* (1969).
3. Frankl, *Man's Search for Meaning*.

Chapter 5   Step 5: Express Negative Feelings

1. Jennifer Warner, "Anxiety Often Missed in Elderly: More Older Adults Affected by Anxiety Disorders Than Depression," *WebMD* (May 22, 2006) http://www.webmd.com/anxiety-panic/guide/20061101/anxiety-missed-elderly.

2. Don Miguel Ruiz, *The Four Agreements: A Practical Guide to Personal Freedom* (San Rafael, California: Amber-Allen Publishing, Inc., 1997).

Chapter 6   Step 6: Take a More Positive View

1. David Watson, "Positive and negative affectivity and their relations to anxiety and depressive disorders," *Journal of Abnormal Psychology* 97 (1988), 346-353.

2. Elaine Fox, *Rainy Brain, Sunny Brain: How to Retrain Your Brain to Overcome Pessimism and Achieve a More Positive Outlook* (New York: Basic Books, 2012).

3. www.coolnsmart.com/3293.

4. Maxine Harris, *The Loss that is Forever* (New York: Dutton, 1995).

5. Erica Goode, "Experts Offer Fresh Insights Into the Mind of the Grieving Child," *The New York Times* (March 28, 2000) http://www.nytimes.com/2000/03/28/health/experts-offer-fresh-insights-into-the-mind-of-the-grieving-child.html.

6. Stacey Burling, "Deathly Difficult: When you know your spouse will die, how do you find the words to tell the kids?" *The Philadelphia Inquirer* (November 28, 2011).

7. W.N. Thetford and R. Walsh, "Theories of Personality and Psychopathology: Schools derived from psychology and philosophy," *Comprehensive Textbook of Psychiatry/IV*, HI Kaplan and BJ Sadock, eds. (Baltimore: Williams & Wilkins, 1985), 459-481.

8. M.P. Duke and S. Nowicki, Jr., "Theories of Personality and Psychopathology: Schools Derived from Psychology and Philosophy," *Comprehensive Textbook of Psychiatry/IV*, H.I. Kaplan and B.J. Sadock, eds., 5th ed. (Baltimore: Williams & Wilkins, 1985), 443-444.

9. Eric Erikson, *Childhood and Society*, 2nd ed. (New York: Norton, 1963).

10. Wendy Lustbader. *Life Gets Better* (New York: Jeremy P. Tarcher/ Penguin, 2011).

11. Ibid., 167.

12. Ibid., 175.

13. Deanne Repich, ed., *Top 100 Inspirational Quotes for Living Anxiety-Free*, Version 1, National Institute of Anxiety and Stress, Inc. (Pflugerville, Texas: 2008), 15, conqueranxiety.com.

Chapter 7   Step 7: Don't Worry

1. Edward M. Hallowell, *Worry: Controlling It and Using It Wisely* (New York: Random House Publishing Group, 1997).

Chapter 8   Step 8: Take Action

1. H Michael Zal, *Panic Disorder: The Great Pretender* (Cambridge, MA: Da Capo Press/Perseus Publishing, 1990).

2. Merriam-Webster.com, http://www.merriam-webster.com/dictionary/agoraphobia.

Chapter 9   Step 9: Take Things as They Are

1. Charles Elliott and Laura Smith, *Overcoming Anxiety for Dummies*, 2nd Ed. (Hoboken, New Jersey: Wiley Publishing, Inc., 2010).

2. Deanne Repich, ed., *Top 100 Inspirational Quotes for Living Anxiety-Free*.

3. Ibid.

4. Eric Berne, *Games People Play* (New York: Grove Press, 1964).

5. Deanne Repich, ed., *Top 100 Inspirational Quotes for Living Anxiety-Free*.

Chapter 11   Therapy

1. Burness E. Moore and Bernard D. Fine, Eds, *A Glossary of Psychoanalytic Terms and Concepts*, 2nd ed. (New York: The American Psychoanalytic Association, 1968).

2. Sebastian Zimmerman, "Intimate Portraits: Psychotherapists in Their Own Work Space," *Psychiatric Times*, Vol. 29: No. 9 (2012): 6.

3. Mark Moran, "Survey Identifies Obstacles to Psychotherapy by Psychiatrists" *Psychiatric News*, Vol. 47, No. 21 (2012), 12.

4. http://www.unitedearth.com.au/proust.html.

5. Phillip Polatin, *A Guide to Treatment in Psychiatry* (Philadelphia: Lippincott, 1966), 100-115.

6. Deanne Repich, ed., *Top 100 Inspirational Quotes for Living Anxiety-Free*.

7. "Maum Meditation, Changing Human Mind To Infinite Universe Mind," Lansdale Maum Meditation Center.

8. www.aapb.org.

9. Harold Kushner, *Conquering Fear: Living Boldly in an Uncertain World* (New York: Anchor Books, 2009), 119.

10. Ibid., 167.

11. Ibid., 24.

Chapter 12   Medication

1. K.L. Granville-Grossman and P. Turner, "The effect of propranolol on anxiety," *Lancet*, Vol. 1 (1966), 788-790.

2. *Physicians' Desk Reference*, 66th ed. (Montvale, NJ: PDR Network, LLC, 2012).

3. Ibid.

4. Ibid.

5. Ibid.

6. Caroline Cassels, "EMA Calls for Withdrawal of Certain Anxiety Medications," *Medscape Psychiatry Report, Medscape News* (2012).

7. *Physicians' Desk Reference*.

8. Ibid.

9. Ibid.

10. Ibid.

11. Ibid.

12. Ibid.

13. Ibid.

14. Ibid.

15. H. Michael Zal, "Herbal Medicine and the Treatment of Anxiety" *Psychiatric Times*, Vol. 17, No. 3, (2000), 63-67.

16. Ibid.

17. Ibid.

18. Ibid.

19. Ibid.

Chapter 13   Anxiety and Adult Attention Deficit Disorder

1. G. Kaplan and J.H. Newcorn, "Pharmacotherapy for children and adolescent attention-deficit hyperactivity disorder," *Pediatric Clinics of North America* 58 (2011), 99-120.

2. www.anxietynomore.co.uk/anxiety-tips.

Chapter 16   Holiday Anxiety

1. www.mdanderson.org.

2. Dan Millman, *The Way of the Peaceful Warrior* (Tiburon, California: HJ Kramer Inc., 1980).

3. Barb Nefer, "Holiday Anxiety," http://www.livestrong.com/article/137093-holiday-anxiety/.

4. Don Miguel Ruiz, *The Four Agreements: A Practical Guide to Personal Freedom* (San Rafael, California: Amber-Allen Publishing, Inc., 1997).

5. G.W. Northup, *Osteopathic Medicine: An American Reformation* (Chicago, Illinois: American Osteoapthic Association, 1966).

6. Leo Buscaglia, *Love* (Thorofare, NJ: Charles B. Slack, Inc., 1972).

Conclusion   The Road to Contentment

1. Art Carey, "Well Being," *The Philadelphia Inquirer* (October 8, 2012).

2. http://www.searchquotes.com/quotation/There_is_no_end_of_craving._Hence_contentment_alone_is_.the_best_way_to_happiness._Therefore,_acquire/221782/.

3. Sonja Lyubomirsky, *The Myths of Happiness* (New York: Penguin Press, 2013).

4. Ibid.

5. John Gray, *Men Are From Mars, Women Are From Venus* (New York: HarperCollins Publishers, Inc., 1992).

6. Don Miguel Ruiz, *The Four Agreements: A Practical Guide to Personal Freedom*.

7. Elizabeth Kubler-Ross and D. Kessler, *Life Lessons* (New York: Scribner, 2001), 31.

8. R.R. Greenson, *The Technique and Practice of Psychoanalysis*, Vol. 1 (New York: International Universities Press, Inc., 1967), 76.

9. "Motivational Quotes from Eternal Optimists," *Reader's Digest* (January 2013) 83, http://www.rd.com/slideshows/motivational-quotes-from-eternal-optimists/#slideshow=slide6.

10. "Do you believe that religious faith can have a positive impact on a patient's outcome?" www.nationalmedpoll.com.

11. Walter Updegrave, "What you really need in retirement: friends," *CNN Money* (February 17, 2010) http://money.cnn.com/2010/02/16/pf/expert/retirement_friendships.moneymag/.

12. Anna Quindlen, *A Short Guide to a Happy Life* (New York: Random House, 2000).